ANATOMY
FOR STRENGTH AND
FITNESS TRAINING

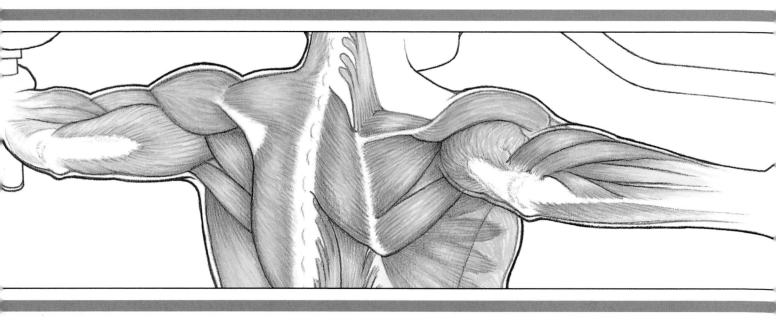

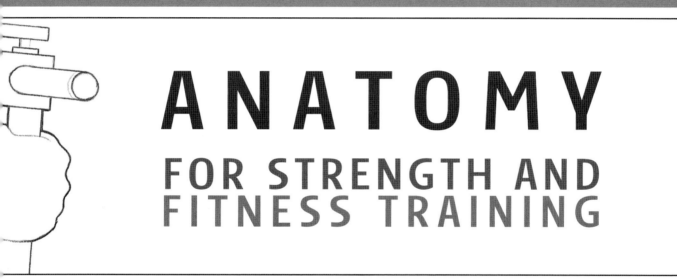

ANATOMY
FOR STRENGTH AND
FITNESS TRAINING

MARK VELLA

McGraw·Hill

New York   Chicago   San Francisco   Lisbon   London   Madrid   Mexico City
Milan   New Delhi   San Juan   Seoul   Singapore   Sydney   Toronto

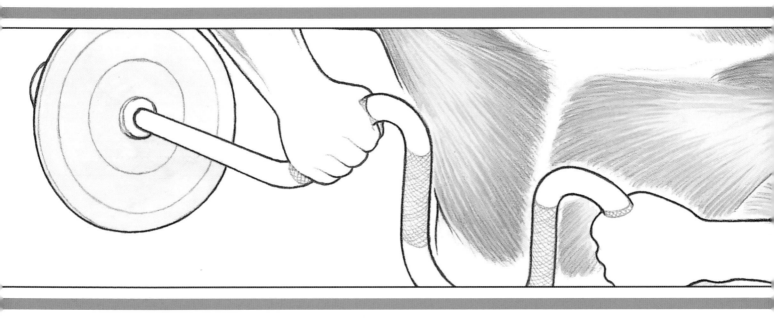

First McGraw-Hill edition, 2006.
Reprinted in 2007.

0 9 8 7 6 5 4

ISBN: 0-07-147533-8

The Library of Congress Cataloging-in-Publication Data is available on file.

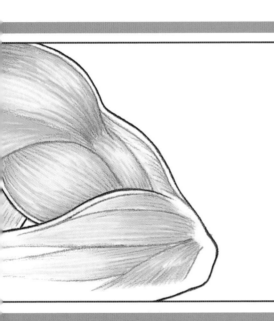

The advice presented within this book requires a knowledge of proper
exercise form and a base level of strength fitness. Although exercise is very
beneficial, the potential for injury does exist, especially if the trainee is not
in good physical condition. Always consult with your physician before
beginning any program of progressive weight training or exercise. If you
feel any strain or pain when you are exercising, stop immediately and
consult your physician. As all systems of weight training involve a systematic
progression of muscular overload, a proper warm-up of muscles, tendons,
ligaments, and joints is mandatory at the beginning of every workout.

McGraw-Hill books are available at special quantity discounts to use as
premiums and sales promotions, or for use in corporate training programs.
For more information, please write to the Director of Special Sales,
Professional Publishing, McGraw-Hill, Two Penn Plaza, New York, NY
10121-2298. Or contact your local bookseller.

Printed in and bound in Singapore.

CONTENTS

HOW TO USE THIS BOOK

Anatomy for Strength and Fitness Training is both a visual and textual analysis of common exercises, and a guide to how to do various exercises properly. The book has two distinct parts: Part One provides a basic introduction to anatomical definitions and terminology. Essentially, it helps to demystify the language used in Part Two, making it easier to follow the instructions in that section.

Part Two contains seven sections: the first four focus on exercises for the chest, legs and hips, back and shoulders, and arms.

Sections five to seven concentrate on exercises to achieve different aims. Section five emphasizes development of the postural stabilizers, section six is devoted to static stretches, and section seven analyzes total body power exercises.

Each section starts with a basic introduction that focuses on the body part or type of training covered. Each exercise is independent, so you can choose the exercises you want to do, and in what sequence.

Within each section, the individual exercises featured are defined and given some background. There is a "how-to" guide for doing the exercise, as well as a visual and technical exercise analysis of which muscles are being used as mobilizers and postural stabilizers. The start and finish position is usually depicted, and training tips may be included.

The adult human body has some 600 muscles and 206 bones; this book looks at about 70 muscles involved in movement and stabilization. Many of the smaller muscles, including the deep, small muscles of the spine, and most muscles of the hands and feet are not given specific attention. If they were, it might well take several pages to analyse just one exercise and movement!

Schematic diagram of how the exercise pages are structured

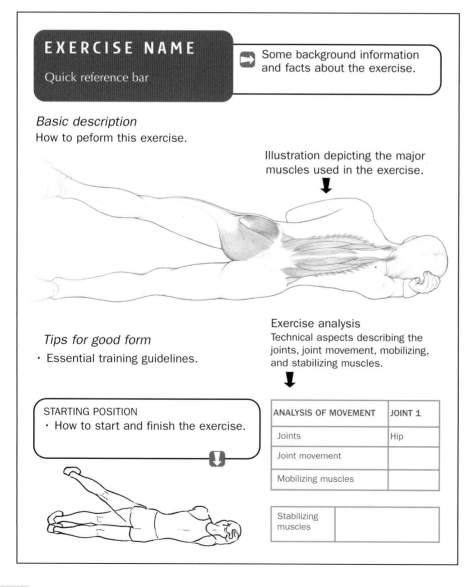

Disclaimer: Many of the exercises have a degree of risk of injury if done without adequate instruction and supervision. We recommend that you get a proper fitness assessment before undertaking any of the exercises, and that you seek qualified instruction if you are a total beginner. This book does not constitute medical advice, and the author and publisher cannot be held liable for any loss, injury, or inconvenience sustained by anyone using this book or the information contained in it.

ANATOMICAL DEFINITIONS AND TERMINOLOGY

Anatomy has its own language and, although technical, it is quite logical, originating mostly from Latin and Greek root words that make it easier to learn and understand the names of muscles, bones, and other body parts.

Whether you are a participant or a qualified exercise practitioner, using the correct terminology makes your work more technically correct and precise, and enables you to interact with other practitioners and work materials.

Like most medical terms, anatomical terms are made up of small word parts, known as combining forms, that fit together to make the full term. These "combining forms" comprise roots, prefixes, and suffixes. Knowing the different word parts allows you to unravel the word. Most anatomical terms only contain two parts: either a prefix and root, or a root and suffix.

For example, if you take the terms subscapular and suprascapular, the root is "scapula," commonly known as the shoulder blades. "Supra" means "above," hence "suprascapular" means something found above the shoulder blades, while "sub" meaning "below" indicates something found below the shoulder blades.

Common prefixes, suffixes, and roots of anatomical terms

Word roots	Meaning	Example	Definition
abdomin	pertaining to the abdomen	abdominal muscle	major muscle group of the abdominal region
acro	extremity	acromion	protruding feature on the scapula bone
articul	pertaining to the joint	articular surface	joint surface
brachi	arm, pertaining to the arm	brachialis	arm muscle
cerv	neck, pertaining to the neck	cervical vertebrae	found in the neck region of the spine
crani	skull	cranium	bones forming the skull
glute	buttock	gluteus maximus	buttock muscle
lig	to tie, to bind	ligament	joins bone to bone
pect, pector	breast, chest	pectoralis major	chest muscle
Word parts used as prefixes			
ab-	away from, from, off	abduction	movement, away from the mid-line
ad-	increase, adherence, toward	adduction	movement, toward the mid-line
ante-, antero-	before, in front	anterior	front aspect of the body
bi-	two, double	bicep brachii	two–headed arm muscle
circum-	around	circumduction	making arm circles
cleido-	the clavicle	sternocleiomastoid	muscle, inserts into clavicle
con-	with, together	concentric contraction	contraction in which muscle attachments move together

Word parts used as prefixes (continued)

Word roots	Meaning	Example	Definition
costo-	rib	costal cartilages	rib cartilages
cune-	wedge	cuneiform	wedge-shaped foot bone
de-	down from, away from, undoing	depression	downward movement of the shoulder blades
dors-	back	dorsiflexion	movement where the "back" or topside of the foot raises up toward the shin
ec-	away from, out of	eccentric contractions	contraction in which muscle attachments move apart
epi-	upon	epicondyle	feature on a bone, located above a condyle
fasci	band	tensor fascia late	small band-like muscle of the hip
flect, flex	bend	flexion	movement, closing the angle of a joint
infra-	below, beneath	infraspinatus muscle	situated below the spine (ridge) of the scapula
meta-	after, behind	metatarsals	bones of the foot, next to the tarsals
post-	after, behind	posterior	rear aspect of the body
pron-	bent forward	prone position	lying face down
proximo	nearest	proximal	directional term, meaning nearest the root of a limb
quadr-	four	quadricep muscle	four-part muscle of the upper thigh
re-	back, again	retraction	movement, pulling the shoulder blades toward the mid-line
serrat-	saw	serratus anterior	muscle with a saw-like edge
sub-	beneath, inferior	subscapularis	muscle beneath the scapula
super, supra-	over, above, excessive	supraspinatus muscle	featured above the spine (ridge) of the scapula
		superior	toward the head
thoraco-	the chest, thorax	thoracic vertebra	in the region of the thorax
trans-	across	transverse abdominus	muscle going across the abdomen, i.e. in the horizontal plane
tri-	three	tricep brachii	three-headed arm muscle
tuber-	swelling	tubercle	small rounded projection on a bone

Word parts used as suffixes

-al, ac	pertaining to	iliac crest	pertaining to the ilium
-cep	head	bicep brachii	two-headed arm muscle
-ic	pertaining to	thoracic vertebra	pertaining to the thorax
-oid	like, in the shape of	rhomboid	upper back muscle, in the shape of a rhomboid
-phragm	partition	diaphragm	muscle separating the thorax and abdomen

SYSTEMS OF THE BODY

The human body can be viewed as an integration of approximately 12 distinct systems that continuously interact to control a multitude of complex functions. These systems are a coordinated assembly of organs, each with specific capabilities, whose tissue structures suit a similar purpose and function.

This book illustrates and analyzes the systems that control movement and posture, namely the muscular and skeletal systems—often referred to jointly as the musculoskeletal system.

The other systems are the cardiovascular, lymphatic, nervous, endocrine, integumentary, respiratory, digestive, urinary, immune/lymphoid, and female and male reproductive systems.

The muscular system

The muscular system facilitates movement, maintenance of posture, and the production of heat and energy. It is made up of three types of muscle tissue: cardiac, smooth, and skeletal.

Cardiac muscle forms the heart walls, while smooth muscle tissue is found in the walls of internal organs such as the stomach and blood vessels. Both are activated involuntarily via the autonomic nervous system and hormonal action.

Skeletal muscle makes up the bulk of the muscles as we commonly know them. The skeletal system includes the tendons that attach muscle to bone, as well as the connective tissue that surrounds and supports the muscle tissue.

A human male weighing 154 lb (70kg) has approximately 55–77 lb (25–35kg) of skeletal muscle.

Muscle attachments

Muscles attach to bone via tendons. The attachment points are referred to as the origin and the insertion.

The origin is the point of attachment that is proximal (closest to the root of a limb), or closest to the mid-line, or center, of the body. It is usually the least moveable point, acting as the anchor in muscle contraction.

The insertion is the point of attachment that is distal (farthest from the root of a limb), or farthest from the mid-line (center) of the body. The insertion is usually the most moveable part, and can be drawn toward the origin.

Knowing the origin and insertion points of a muscle, which joint or joints the muscle crosses, and what movement it causes at that joint/joints is a key element of the exercise analysis.

There are typical features on all bones that act as convenient attachment points for the muscles. Because these attachment points feature prominently in the muscle tables at the start of each section in Part Two, a description of typical bone features is given in the table on p14.

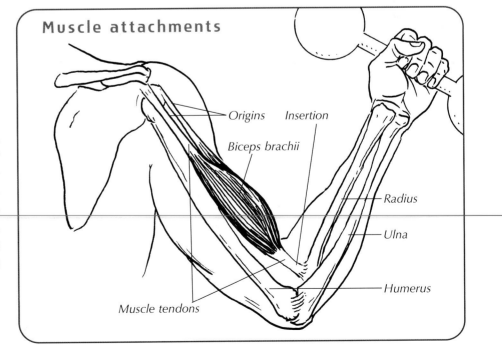

Muscle attachments

Origins · Insertion · Biceps brachii · Radius · Ulna · Humerus · Muscle tendons

The muscular system

Anterior view

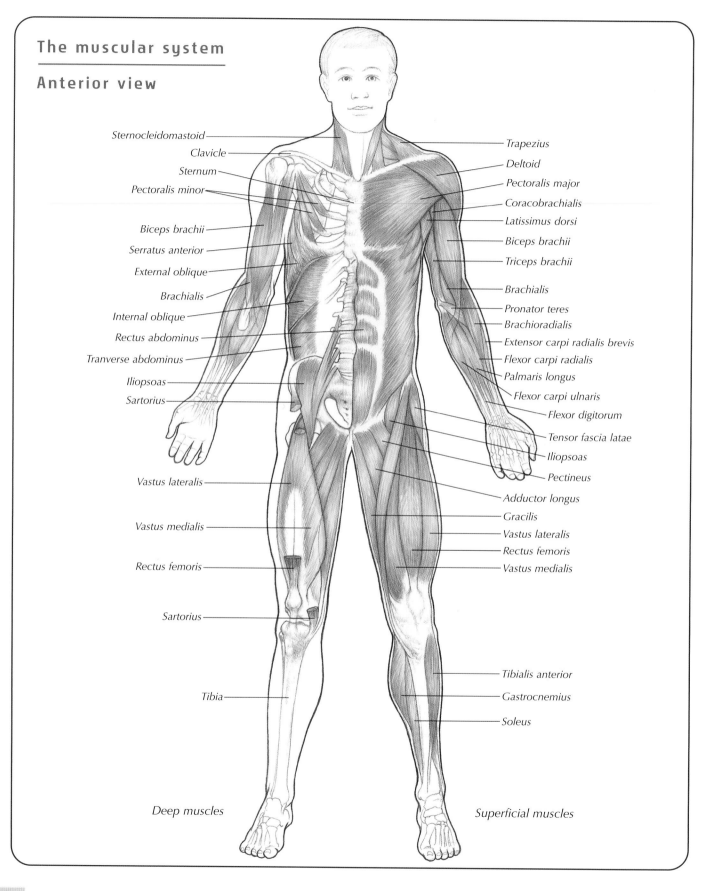

Sternocleidomastoid

Clavicle

Sternum

Pectoralis minor

Biceps brachii

Serratus anterior

External oblique

Brachialis

Internal oblique

Rectus abdominus

Tranverse abdominus

Iliopsoas

Sartorius

Vastus lateralis

Vastus medialis

Rectus femoris

Sartorius

Tibia

Deep muscles

Trapezius

Deltoid

Pectoralis major

Coracobrachialis

Latissimus dorsi

Biceps brachii

Triceps brachii

Brachialis

Pronator teres

Brachioradialis

Extensor carpi radialis brevis

Flexor carpi radialis

Palmaris longus

Flexor carpi ulnaris

Flexor digitorum

Tensor fascia latae

Iliopsoas

Pectineus

Adductor longus

Gracilis

Vastus lateralis

Rectus femoris

Vastus medialis

Tibialis anterior

Gastrocnemius

Soleus

Superficial muscles

The muscular system

Posterior view

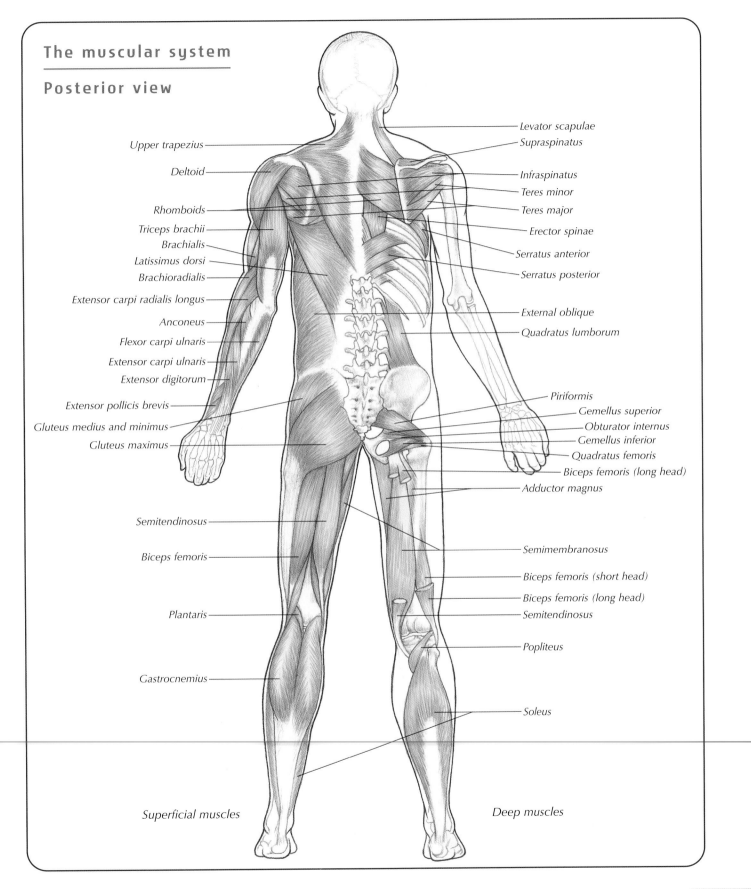

Levator scapulae
Supraspinatus
Upper trapezius
Infraspinatus
Deltoid
Teres minor
Teres major
Rhomboids
Erector spinae
Triceps brachii
Brachialis
Serratus anterior
Latissimus dorsi
Serratus posterior
Brachioradialis
Extensor carpi radialis longus
External oblique
Anconeus
Quadratus lumborum
Flexor carpi ulnaris
Extensor carpi ulnaris
Extensor digitorum
Piriformis
Extensor pollicis brevis
Gemellus superior
Gluteus medius and minimus
Obturator internus
Gluteus maximus
Gemellus inferior
Quadratus femoris
Biceps femoris (long head)
Adductor magnus
Semitendinosus
Semimembranosus
Biceps femoris
Biceps femoris (short head)
Biceps femoris (long head)
Plantaris
Semitendinosus
Popliteus
Gastrocnemius
Soleus

Superficial muscles

Deep muscles

Typical features on a bone

Feature	Description	Examples
Condyle	Large, rounded projection at a joint that usually articulates with another bone	· Medial and lateral condyle of the femur · Lateral condyle of the tibia
Epicondyle	Projection located above a condyle	Medial or lateral epicondyle of the humerus
Facet	Small, flat joint surfaces	Facet joints of the vertebra
Head	Significant, rounded projection at the proximal end of a bone, usually forming a joint	Head of the humerus
Crest	Ridge-like, narrow projection	Iliac crest of the pelvis
Line, Linea	Lesser significant ridge, running along a bone	Linea aspera of the femur
Process	Any significant projection	· Coracoid and acromion process of the scapula · Olecranon process of the ulna at the elbow joint
Spine, Spinous process	Significant, slender projection away from the surface of the bone	· Spinous processes of the vertebra · Spine of the scapula
Suture	Joint line between two bones forming a fixed or semi-fixed joint	Sutures that join the bones of the skull
Trochanter	Very large projection	Greater trochanter of the femur
Tubercle	Small, rounded projection	Greater tubercles of the humerus
Tuberosity	Large, rounded, or roughened projection	Ischial tuberosities on the pelvis, commonly known as the "sitting bones"
Foramen	Rounded hole or opening in a bone	The vertebral foramen running down the length of the spine, in which the spinal cord is housed
Fossa	Hollow, shallow, or flattened surface on a bone	Supraspinous and infraspinous fossa on the scapula

The word "skeleton" originates from a Greek word meaning "dried up." Infants are born with about 350 bones, many of which fuse as they grow, forming single bones, resulting in the 206 bones an adult has.

The skeletal system

This consists of our bones, ligaments (which join bone to bone), and joints. Joints are referred to as articulations and are sometimes classified as a separate system, the articular system.

Apart from facilitating movement, the primary functions of the skeletal system include supporting the muscles, protecting the soft tissues and inner organs, the storage of surplus minerals, and the formation of red blood cells in the bone marrow of the long bones.

Integrated systems

The body's systems are completely and intricately interdependent. For movement to take place, for example, the respiratory system brings in oxygen and the digestive system breaks down our food into essential nutrients, both of which the cardiovascular system then carries to the working muscles via the blood to facilitate the energy reactions that result in physical work being done.

The lymphatic and circulatory systems help to carry away the waste products of these energy reactions, which are later converted and/or excreted by the digestive and urinary systems. The nervous system interacts with the muscles to facilitate the contraction and relaxation of muscle tissue. The articular system of joints allows the levers of the body to move.

The femur (thigh bone) is about one-quarter of a person's height. It is also the largest, heaviest, and strongest bone in the body. The shortest bone, the stirrup bone in the ear, is only about 2.5mm long. An adult's skeleton weighs about 20 lb (9kg).

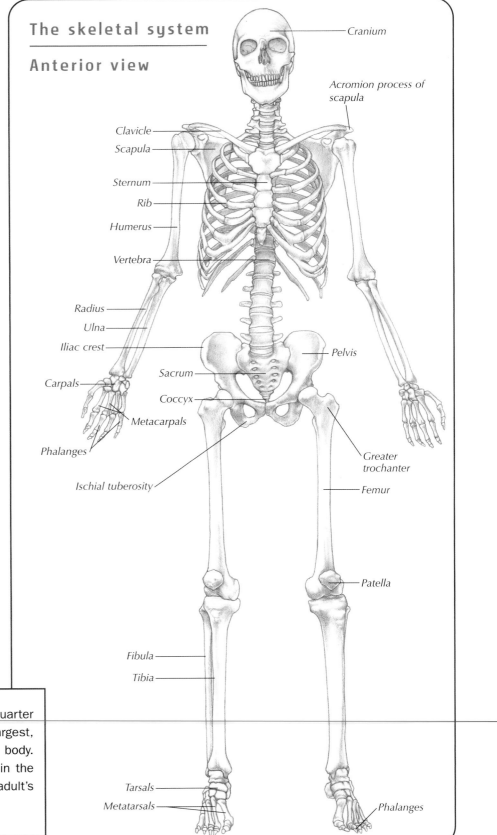

The skeletal system

Anterior view

Cranium

Acromion process of scapula

Clavicle

Scapula

Sternum

Rib

Humerus

Vertebra

Radius

Ulna

Iliac crest

Carpals

Sacrum

Coccyx

Metacarpals

Phalanges

Pelvis

Greater trochanter

Femur

Ischial tuberosity

Patella

Fibula

Tibia

Tarsals

Metatarsals

Phalanges

BODY PLANES AND REGIONS

When learning anatomy and analyzing movement, we refer to a standard reference position of the human body, known as the anatomical position. All movements, and the location of the anatomical structures, are named as if the person was standing in this position (see illustration below left).

Regional anatomy

This book is a technical labeling guide to the different superficial parts of the body. In anatomical language, common names such as "head" are replaced by anatomical terms derived from Latin, such as "cranial" or "cranium."

Within the different body regions there are sub-regions. For example, within the cranial region are the frontal, occipital, parietal, and temporal subregions.

Anatomical planes

The human body can be divided into three imaginary planes of reference, each perpendicular to the other.

The sagittal plane passes through the body from the front to the back, dividing it into a right half and a left half. The mid-line of the body is called the median. If the body is divided in the sagittal plane, directly though the median, this is known as the median sagittal plane.

The coronal (frontal) plane passes through the body from the top of the head to bottom of the feet, dividing the body into front and back sections.

The transverse (horizontal) plane passes through the middle of the body at right angles, dividing it into a top and a bottom section.

An anatomical cross-section of the internal structures of the body can be viewed in any one of these planes, which are also described as "planes of motion," as the joint movements are defined in relation to one of the three planes. Understanding which plane an anatomical cross-section is divided into will help you know what you are looking at, and from which viewpoint.

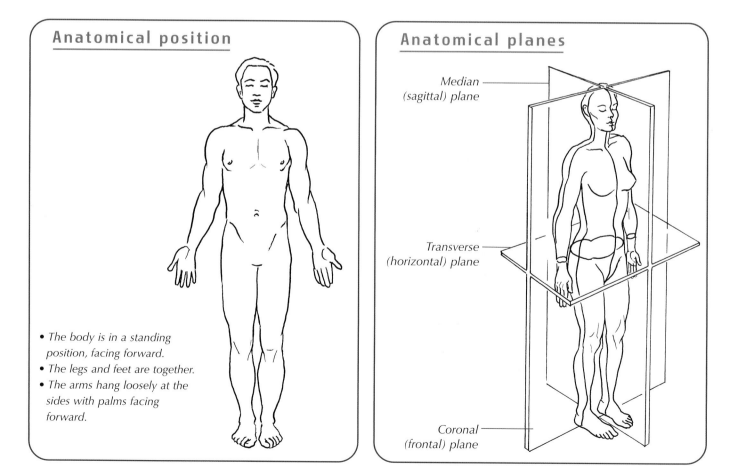

Anatomical position

- *The body is in a standing position, facing forward.*
- *The legs and feet are together.*
- *The arms hang loosely at the sides with palms facing forward.*

Anatomical planes

Median (sagittal) plane

Transverse (horizontal) plane

Coronal (frontal) plane

ANATOMY FOR STRENGTH AND FITNESS TRAINING

ANATOMICAL TERMS

There are standard anatomical terms which describe the position or direction of one structure of the body and its relationship to other structures or parts of the body.

The human body is a complex, three-dimensional structure; knowing the proper anatomical terms of position and direction will help you to compare one point on the body with another, and understand where it is situated in relation to other anatomical features.

These terms are standard, regardless of whether the person is sitting, standing, or lying down, and are named as if the person was standing in the anatomical position (see opposite page). Terms of direction should not be confused with joint movements (see pp 18–20).

Anatomical terms of position and direction

Position	Definition	Example of usage
Anterior	Toward the front, pertaining to the front	The abdominal muscles are found on the anterior aspect of the body
Posterior	Toward the back, pertaining to the rear	The hamstring muscles are situated on the posterior aspect of the leg
Superior	Above another structure, toward the head	The shoulder is superior to the hip
Inferior	Below another structure, toward the feet	The hip is inferior to the shoulder
Lateral	Away from the mid-line, on or toward the outside	The outside of the knee joint is its lateral aspect
Medial	Toward the mid-line of the body, pertaining to the middle or center	The inside of the knee joint is its medial aspect
Proximal	Closest to the trunk, or root of a limb. Also sometimes used to refer to the origin of a muscle	The hip joint is proximal to the knee
Distal	Situated away from the mid-line or center of the body, or root of a limb. Also sometimes used to refer to a point away from the origin of a muscle	The toes are the most distal part of the leg
Superficial	Closer to the surface of the body, more toward the surface of the body than another structure	The Rectus femoris is the most superficial of the quadricep muscles
Deep	Farther from the surface, relatively deeper into the body than another structure	The heart is deep compared with the ribs that protect it
Prone	Lying face downward	Prone Lying Back Extensions (see p70) are done, as the name suggests, from a prone lying starting position
Supine	Lying on the back, face upward	The Abdominal Crunch exercise (see p109) is performed from a supine lying starting position

JOINT MOVEMENT

Knowing and understanding movement (which joint is moving, how it moves), is essential in order to be able to analyze a complex exercise. This book has done the task of joint identification for you, and understanding this section will help improve your exercise analysis.

Types of joints

Some joints are fixed or semi-fixed, allowing little or no movement. For instance, the skull bones join together in structures known as sutures to form fixed joints; but where the spine joins the pelvis, the sacroiliac joint is semi-fixed and allows minimal movement ("sacro" from sacrum and "iliac" pertaining to the pelvic crest).

A third category, called synovial joints, are free-moving joints, and move in different ways determined by their particular shape, size, and structure.

Synovial joints are the most common joints in the body. They are characterized by a joint capsule that surrounds the articulation, the inner membrane of which secretes lubricating synovial fluid, stimulated by movement. Typical synovial joints include the shoulder, knee, hip, ankle, the joints of the feet and hands, and the vertebral joints.

Joint action

When performing an activity such as lifting weights or running, the combination of nerve stimulation and muscular contraction facilitates the movement that occurs at the synovial joints.

When doing a Bicep curl, for example (see p96), the weight rises because the angle of the elbow joint closes as the bicep muscles, which attach from the upper arm bones to the radius and ulna, shorten in contraction, thereby lifting the forearm.

Joint movement pointers

Most joint movements have common names that apply to most major joints, but there are some movements that only occur at one specific joint.

The common joint movements occur in similar anatomical planes of motion. For example, shoulder, hip, and knee flexion all occur in the sagittal plane (see p16). This makes it logical and easier to learn about joint movements and movement analysis.

In the accompanying table (see below and opposite page), common movements are listed first, followed by specific movements that only occur at one joint.

Strictly speaking, it is incorrect to name only the movement and a limb or body part. For example, "leg extension" does not clarify whether this happens at the knee, hip, or ankle. Get into the habit of always pairing the movement with the joint that is moved, for example: shoulder flexion, knee extension, spinal rotation, scapular depression, and so on. (Possibly the only exception to this is when referring to trunk movements, when all the joints of the spine combine to create movement of the whole body part.)

Movements generally occur in pairs. For every movement, there must be a return movement to the starting position. Typical pairs are flexion and extension, abduction and adduction, internal rotation and external rotation, protraction and retraction (see p20). You will notice these pairs when you look at the exercise analyses in Part Two which follows.

Remember, all movements are named as if the person was standing in the anatomical position (see p16). So "elbow flexion" will be the same regardless of whether you are standing up, lying down (supine), or in a sitting position.

Major joint movements

General movements	Plane	Description	Example
Abduction	Coronal	Movement away from the mid-line	Hip abduction (see p54)
Adduction	Coronal	Movement toward the mid-line	Hip adduction (see p53)
Flexion	Sagittal	Decreasing the angle between two structures	Moving the forearm toward the upper arm. Standing Barbell Curl (see p94)
Extension	Sagittal	Increasing the angle between two structures	Moving the forearm away from the upper arm. As above, downward phase (see p94)
Medial rotation (internal rotation)	Transverse	Turning around the vertical axis of a bone toward the mid-line	Cable Crossover (see p36)

Lateral rotation (external/ outward rotation)	Transverse	Turning around the vertical axis of a bone away from the mid-line	Turning at the waist
Circumduction	All planes	Complete circular movement at shoulder or hip joints	Swinging your arms in circles

Specific movements			

1. Ankle movements			
Plantarflexion	Sagittal	Moving the foot downward	Machine Standing Calf Raises (upward phase, see p58)
Dorsiflexion (Dorsal flexion)	Sagittal	Moving the foot toward the shin	Machine Standing Calf Raises (downward phase, see p58)

2. Forearm movements (the radioulnar joint)			
Pronation	Transverse	Rotating the wrist and hand medially from the elbow	Seated Dumb-bell Curl (See p95)
Supination	Transverse	Rotating the wrist and hand laterally from the elbow	Making circular movements with your hand

3. Scapula movements			
Depression	Coronal	Movement of the scapulae inferiorly, e.g. squeezing scapulae downward	To stabilize the shoulder girdle e.g. Hip Flexor Apparatus (see p111)
Elevation	Coronal	Movement of the scapulae superiorly, e.g. hunching the shoulders	Dumb-bell Shoulder Shrugs (see p82)
Abduction (protraction)	Transverse	Movement of the scapulae away from the spine	Seated Low Cable Pulley Rows (see p68)
Adduction (retraction)	Transverse	Movement of the scapulae toward the spine	As above
Downward rotation (medial rotation)	Coronal	Scapulae rotate downward, in the return from upward rotation	Machine Cable Front Lat Pull-down (see p62)
Upward rotation (lateral rotation)	Coronal	Scapulae rotate upward. The inferior border of the scapulae move laterally and upward	As above (see p62)

4. Shoulder movements			
Horizontal abduction/extension (transverse abduction)	Transverse	Movement of the humerus across the body away from the mid-line	Dumb-bell Flat Bench Flyes (see p34)
Horizontal adduction/flexion (transverse adduction)	Transverse	Movement of the humerus across the body toward the mid-line	As above (see p34)

5. Spine/trunk movements			
Lateral flexion	Coronal	Movement of the trunk away from the mid-line in the coronal plane.	Dumb-bell Side Bends (see p107)
Reduction (adduction/return)	Coronal	Return of the trunk to the mid-line in the coronal plane	As above (see p107)

6. Wrist movements			
Flexion (palmar flexion)	Sagittal	The hand moves toward the anterior surface of the forearm	Barbell Wrist Curls (see p98)
Extension (dorsal flexion/ dorsiflexion)	Sagittal	The hand moves toward the posterior surface of the forearm	Reverse Barbell Wrist Curls (see p99)

Joint movements

The knee joint is the largest, the hip joint is the strongest, and the shoulder is potentially the most unstable joint in the body.

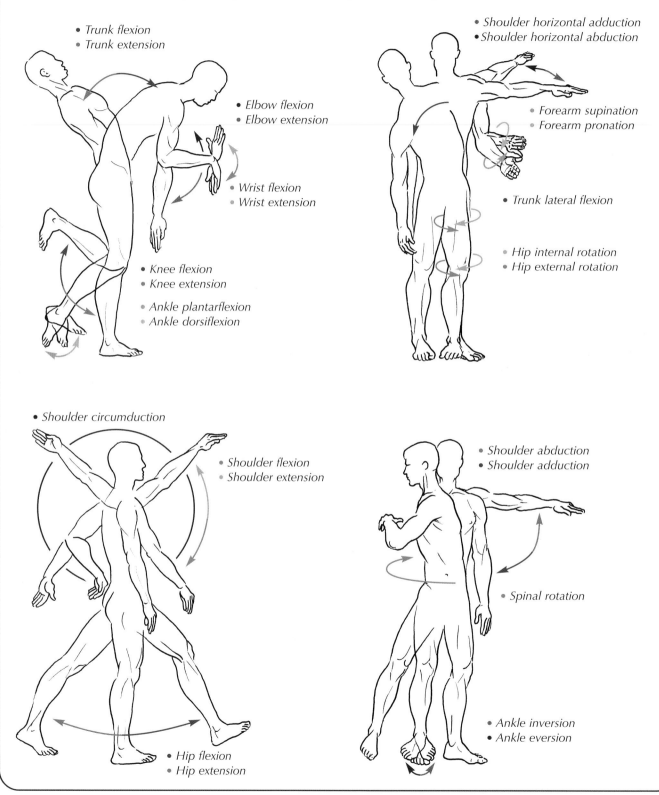

- *Trunk flexion*
- *Trunk extension*

- *Elbow flexion*
- *Elbow extension*

- *Wrist flexion*
- *Wrist extension*

- *Knee flexion*
- *Knee extension*

- *Ankle plantarflexion*
- *Ankle dorsiflexion*

- *Shoulder horizontal adduction*
- *Shoulder horizontal abduction*

- *Forearm supination*
- *Forearm pronation*

- *Trunk lateral flexion*

- *Hip internal rotation*
- *Hip external rotation*

- *Shoulder circumduction*

- *Shoulder flexion*
- *Shoulder extension*

- *Hip flexion*
- *Hip extension*

- *Shoulder abduction*
- *Shoulder adduction*

- *Spinal rotation*

- *Ankle inversion*
- *Ankle eversion*

ANATOMY FOR STRENGTH AND FITNESS TRAINING

POSTURE AND MUSCLE BALANCE

Many of the exercises and machines depicted in this book originate from the bodybuilding culture, which focuses on strength and weight gain, but most of us require a balance of strength from our training, as well as useful functionality of that strength for day-to-day living—hence the term "functional exercise."

Functional exercise

The SAID principle (Specific Adaptation to Imposed Demands) describes the training dictum that our bodies will predictably change in response to the demands that are placed on them, and is one of the basic tenets of strength training and conditioning.

For example, if I cycle regularly, I will become a better cyclist, not a better runner. This illustrates why it is important to train your body in postures, or functional positions, and in a way that is close to the demands of your daily life.

Exercising in standing positions, for example, strengthens the spine and trunk, and leg stabilizers, contributing to their fitness for everyday activities.

This does not mean that training in a gym has to be boring and rigid. Not at all; it is about incorporating functional principles into your training regime. Nor does functional training in a gym negate the need to practice the principles of good posture and alignment, as well as safe and effective positions and movement when not in the gym.

One way to make an exercise more functional is to perform it "weight bearing," that is, standing. However, if you are a beginner, or want to isolate a particular muscle, it may be better to start in a sitting position. Another effective way to make an exercise functional is to make it compound, as opposed to isolated. This means working more than one major muscle group at a

time. It also implies working stabilizers and mobilizers (see p23) together in one exercise.

Closed and open chain exercise

Another concept often referred to in functional exercise is whether an exercise is regarded as "open" or "closed" chain. These terms reputedly come from the work of orthopedic specialist Dr Arthur Steindler (*Kinesiology of the Human Body*) in which he states: "In open chain joint movements, the proximal muscle attachment or body part is fixed, while the distal member moves (for example, reaching to grasp an object or kicking a ball). In a closed chain joint motion, the distal muscle attachment or body part is fixed or stable, and the proximal part moves (rising from a chair or performing a pull-up, for example)."

Pelvic positions

| Neutral pelvic alignment | Anterior tilt | Posterior tilt |

In gym circles, closed kinetic chain exercises are usually defined as movements which have either a hand or foot, or both, grounded so the body forms a closed chain (as in a squat). By Steindler's definition then, a barbell bicep curl would be considered open chain, although it is usually referred to as closed chain.

This book defines exercises according to Steindler's terms (see the Quick Reference bar for each exercise).

Differences aside, however, exercise positions that form a closed chain with the ground are generally regarded as more functional, more stable, and, often, more suitable for those who are less fit. Closed chain exercises have broad applications in general training and the rehabilitation of injuries.

Posture and alignment

The line of gravity—the gravitational pull that the earth exerts on a body—acts through the body in a straight line toward the earth's center.

In a standing position, neutral alignment occurs when body landmarks, such as the ankles, knees, hips, and shoulders, are in line with the pull of gravity. The body is balanced front to back and side to side, allowing it to maintain position against gravity with minimal effort. The curves of the spine are balanced. Seen from the lateral aspect, the ear, shoulder, hip, knee, and ankle all fall within the plumb-line.

In neutral alignment, the pelvis is in a neutral position with the pubic ramus and superior anterior iliac crest vertically aligned (see p21). In this position, if the pelvis was a bucket of water, no water would spill out to any side. With an anterior tilt of the pelvis, the water spills out in front; with a posterior tilt, the water spills to the back.

As we exercise and move the body in different positions, such as squats or push-ups, gravity continues to act, the critical points of balance shift, and we have to work harder to maintain balance and alignment. (Spinal alignment occurs whether a person is lying, sitting, or at an angle, and is named as if in the anatomical position.) When told to "maintain a neutral spine," as in a squat, for example, the ear, shoulder, hip, and pelvis should remain in alignment (just not in a vertical line).

Poor postural control and alignment affect your quality of movement and the safety and effectiveness of any exercise, as postural compensation is likely to occur. This means that the joints used, joint actions, range of movement, and involvement of the various stabilizing and mobilizing muscles, will change from the ideal presented in the exercise analyses.

An example would be doing the Standing Barbell Curl (see p94) incorrectly: "cheating" by using momentum generated in the lower back to help lift the bar (evidenced by rocking back and forth). Because postural stabilization ability is not adequate for the chosen weight, it will result in a reduced range of movement at the elbow joint and, subsequently, reduced use of the bicep muscle. Additionally, because the lower back is unstable, the abdominal muscles, which work as postural stabilizers, will disengage and not be trained effectively, increasing the risk of injury to the lower back.

Stabilizers and mobilizers

One common classification of muscles is by whether they are performing a stabilizing or mobilizing function.

A mobilizer is a muscle primarily responsible for movement, such as the biceps muscles performing the motion of a barbell curl.

Stabilizers are muscles whose prime purpose in the body, or in a given movement is to maintain the stability and alignment of the rest of the body, so that the effective movement can be performed by the mobilizing muscles.

For example, in a Standing Barbell Curl (see p94), the rotator cuff muscles stabilize and align the shoulder joint, and the abdominal group maintains the alignment of the spine, while the biceps group performs the isotonic contraction. Certain muscles, by virtue of their position, shape, angle, and structure, are more suited to work as stabilizers than as mobilizers.

The abdominal group is one of several major stabilizers highlighted in this book. Other muscles that perform stabilizing functions include the gluteus and hamstring groups, *Tensor fascia latae*, *Rectus femoris*, *Iliopsoas*, the adductor group, *Tibialis posterior* in the legs and hips, *Erector spinae*, *Serratus anterior*, lower and mid trapezius, Rhomboids, and rotator cuff group in the back and shoulders.

Neutral alignment is maintained by opposing pairs of stabilizing muscles which balance us in each plane (front to back, side to side etc.).

In functional fitness training (geared toward the requirements of day-to-day living), we want to train muscles in the way they were naturally intended to work; that is, to use stabilizers as stabilizers, and mobilizers as mobilizers. However, if you are using an exercise machine that supports the body (particularly seated, prone, supine, or leaning types) you are not necessarily using your body's stabilizer systems. Stability must always come before force, so when you use exercise machines, ensure that you pay attention to stabilizing your posture and obtaining good alignment as you work.

Training goals for various exercise programs

	FREQUENCY (per week)	DURATION	LOAD (on a scale of 1–10)	REPETITIONS	NUMBER OF SETS	REST PERIODS
Novice	2	20–45 min	5–7	8–12	1–2	30–60 sec
Weight loss	2–4	15–30 min *	4–6	15–30	1–2	15–30 sec
Cardiovascular endurance	2–4	15–30 min *	5–7	12–25	1–3	15–60 sec
Muscular endurance	3–5	20–45 min	3–8	12–30	2–3	30–120 sec
Muscle tone	3–5	20–45 min	6–7.5	12–15	2–3	30–120 sec
Hypertrophy **	3–6	40–75 min	7–8.5	6–12	4–6	30–90 sec
Strength **	3–6	40–75 min	8–10	1–8	4–5	2–8 min
Power **	3–6	20–45 min	3–9	1–6	4–5	2–8 min

* This does not allow for time spent doing cardiovascular exercise (e.g. running or cycling), as part of the program goals.
** Advanced programs which may require initial supervision.
See p130 for some sample exercise programs.

PRACTICING EXERCISE ANALYSIS

Movement analysis (analyzing an exercise), enables you to understand what joints and muscles are used in a certain movement and how they are moving. Changing a movement, or doing it incorrectly, affects both the muscles used to perform the exercise and how they are used. Exercise analysis can help you to determine if the muscles you intend to train are utilized in a specific exercise, as well as whether you are doing it correctly. It is therefore an essential skill in understanding exercise programing.

There are numerous ways of analyzing an exercise. One simple but effective method, which is used in this book, is based on a series of questions (see below). Exercise analysis can also be applied to static positions, such as yoga postures or stretches, where holding a joint at a particular angle will result in some muscles being stretched and/or others being activated to stabilize the position.

When analyzing an exercise, the three most important questions to consider are:
· What joint or joints are moving?
· How are they moving (flexion, extension etc.)?
· What muscles cause those specific movements?

Other questions that help to break down an exercise include:
· What muscles are being used to stabilize the posture during exercise?
· How can I progress, regress, or vary this exercise?

OVERVIEW OF ANATOMY

CHEST EXERCISES

GENERAL GUIDELINES FOR STRENGTH TRAINING

· Allow time for a proper warm-up, especially of muscles to be worked during a specific training session.

· Train consistently and progress slowly. It takes three months for muscles and joints to adapt to new training.

· Set your training frequency to your level of experience and ability (2–3 days a week for novices, more for advanced).

· Use compound muscle group exercises before isolation ones, and train larger muscle groups before smaller ones.

· Good form (technique) is important. Stability should precede force generation.

· Learn the difference between "good pain" (training effort) and "bad pain" (injury). The latter is a warning sign that should not be ignored.

· Use full range of motion.

· Breathe consistently and avoid holding your breath.

· Vary your training, both the type of exercise as well as the duration and intensity of exercise sessions.

Muscles involved in chest exercises

Name	Joints crossed	Origin	Insertion	Action
Pectoralis major	Shoulder	· Clavicular (upper portion): medial half of the anterior surface of the clavicle · Sternal (mid-portion) and abdominal (lower) portion · Anterior surface of the costal cartilages of the first six ribs and the adjoining portion of the sternum	Flat tendon of the intertubercular groove of the humerus	Shoulder: · adduction · horizontal adduction · internal rotation · flexion
Pectoralis minor	Scapula to ribs	Anterior surface of the third to the fifth ribs	Coracoid process of the scapula	Scapula: · abduction (protraction) · downward rotation · depression
Anterior deltoid	Shoulder	Anterior lateral third of the clavicle	Lateral side of the humerus	Shoulder: · flexion · horizontal flexion · medial rotation
Triceps brachii	Shoulder and elbow	Scapula and upper posterior humerus	The olecranon process of the ulna	Elbow extension
Serratus anterior	Shoulder	Upper nine ribs at the side of the chest	Anterior aspect of the entire medial border of the scapula	Scapula: · abduction (protraction) · upward rotation
Coracobrachialis	Shoulder	Coracoid process of the scapula	Middle medial border of humeral shaft	Shoulder: · horizontal adduction
Anconeus	Elbow	Posterior lateral condyle of the humerus	Posterior surface of the olecranon process of the ulna	Elbow extension (works with the triceps)

Note: The Triceps brachii is detailed under Arms (see p85).

Chest muscles

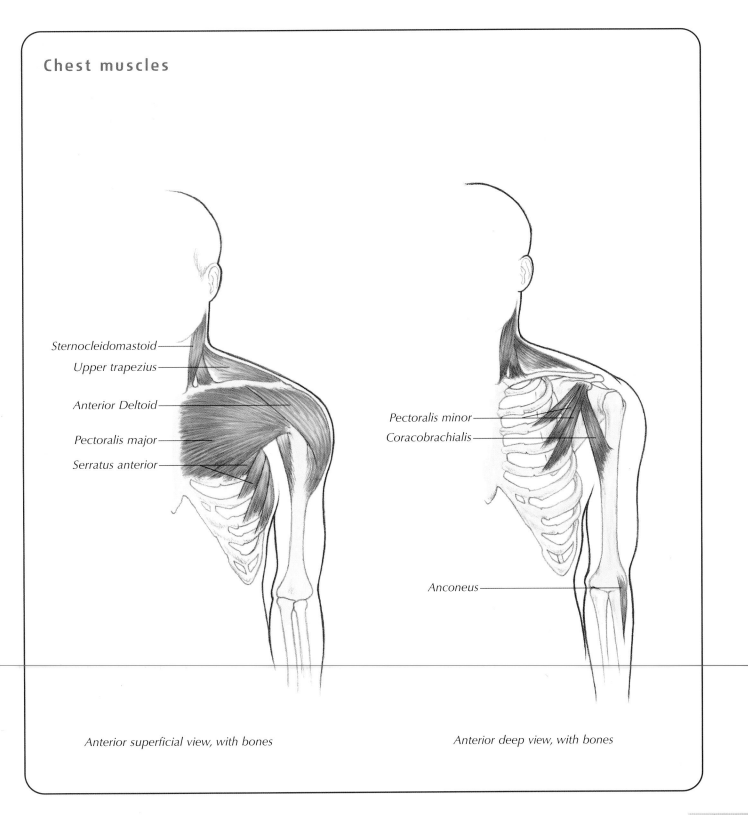

Sternocleidomastoid

Upper trapezius

Anterior Deltoid

Pectoralis major

Serratus anterior

Pectoralis minor

Coracobrachialis

Anconeus

Anterior superficial view, with bones

Anterior deep view, with bones

BARBELL BENCH PRESS

Core exercise • Compound/multi-joint
• Push • Open chain • Barbell
• Intermediate to advanced

In the "Strongest Man in the World" competition, Anthony Clark from the Philippines, bench-pressed a massive 800 lb (363kg). Since he weighs 350 lb (159kg), that's nearly 2½ times his own body-weight!

Basic description

Dismount bar from rack. Bending the elbows, lower the bar in line with the upper chest. Return by pressing upward until arms are extended. Repeat.

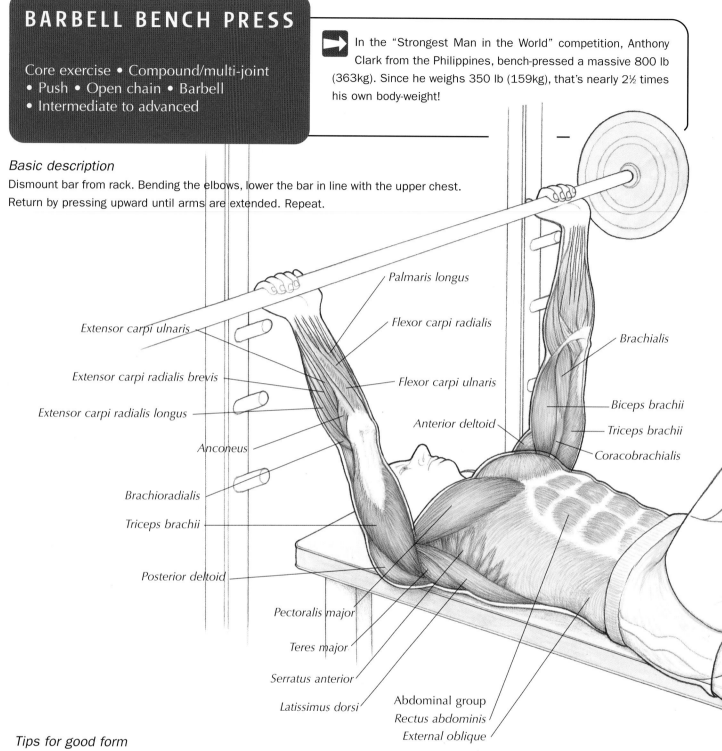

Palmaris longus

Flexor carpi radialis

Brachialis

Extensor carpi ulnaris

Extensor carpi radialis brevis

Flexor carpi ulnaris

Biceps brachii

Extensor carpi radialis longus

Anterior deltoid

Triceps brachii

Anconeus

Coracobrachialis

Brachioradialis

Triceps brachii

Posterior deltoid

Pectoralis major

Teres major

Serratus anterior

Latissimus dorsi

Abdominal group
Rectus abdominis
External oblique

Tips for good form

· Get good form before increasing weight.
· Avoid momentum; use slow, controlled motion.
· Breathe out when raising the bar.

ANATOMY FOR STRENGTH AND FITNESS TRAINING

ANALYSIS OF MOVEMENT	JOINT 1	JOINT 2	JOINT 3
Joints	Elbow	Shoulder	Scapulothoracic
Joint movement	Up—extension Down—flexion	Up—horizontal adduction, flexion Down—horizontal abduction, extension	Up—partial upward rotation, abduction Down—partial downward rotation, adduction
Mobilizing muscles	Triceps brachii Anconeus	Pectoralis major, emphasis on the sternal and clavicular aspect Coracobrachialis Anterior deltoid	Serratus anterior

Stabilizing muscles	Shoulder blades: Serratus anterior, Pectoralis minor, lower Trapezius Shoulder joint: Rotator cuff muscles, Biceps brachii Mid-trunk stabilization: Abdominal and Gluteal group, Rhomboids, Lower trapezius, Latissimus dorsi

STARTING POSITION
· Lying supine.
· Medium grip (slightly wider than shoulder-width).
· Spine aligned (if appropriate, raise feet onto the bench to reduce arching in the lower back).

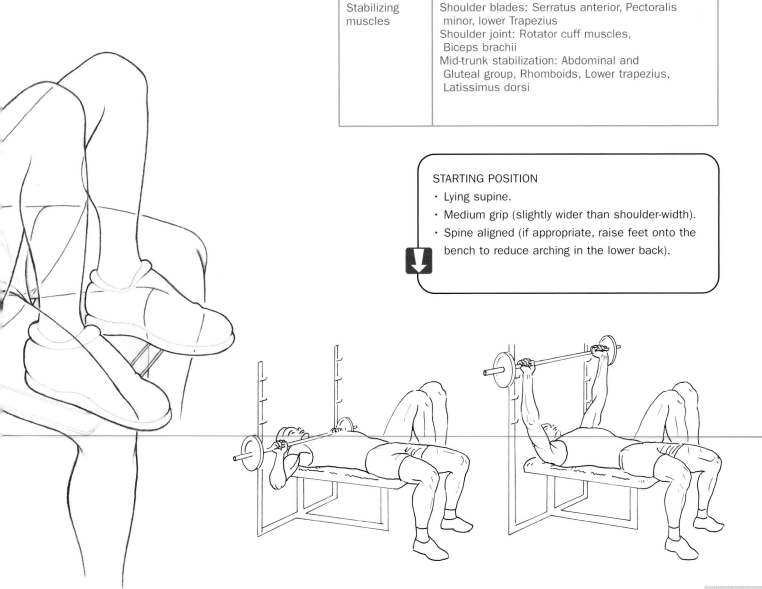

PUSH-UPS

Core exercise • Compound/ multi-joint
• Push • Close chain • Body-weight
• Functional • Beginner to advanced

➡️ Paddy Doyle of the UK currently holds the Guinness World Record for the most push-ups done in one year (1988–89), a phenomenal 1,500,230!

Basic description

Maintaining posture, lower the body to the floor by bending the elbows. Return by pushing the body up until the arms are straight and the elbows are extended. Repeat.

Tips for good form

· Use slow, controlled movement.
· Maintain spinal alignment.
· Avoid compensating with momentum.

ANALYSIS OF MOVEMENT	JOINT 1	JOINT 2	JOINT 3
Joints	Elbow	Shoulder	Scapulothoracic
Joint movement	Up—extension Down—flexion	Up—horizontal adduction, flexion Down—horizontal abduction, extension	Up—partial upward rotation, abduction Down—partial downward rotation, adduction
Mobilizing muscles	Triceps brachii Anconeus	Pectoralis major, emphasis on the sternal and clavicular aspect Coracobrachialis Anterior deltoid	Serratus anterior

Stabilizing muscles	A stronger stabilization emphasis than in the bench press (see pp 26–27) Shoulder blades: Serratus anterior, Pectoralis minor, Rhomboids, lower Trapezius Shoulder joint: Rotator cuff muscles, Biceps brachii Trunk stabilization: Abdominal, Gluteal, and Quadricep group, Quadratus lumborum, Latissimus dorsi

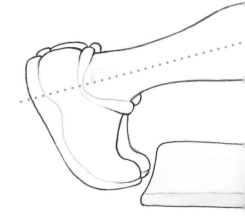

⟶

STARTING POSITION
· Lying prone.
· Raise up body, supported on hands and toes.
· Extend arms, keeping them slightly wider than shoulder-width at upper chest level.
· Keep posture aligned.

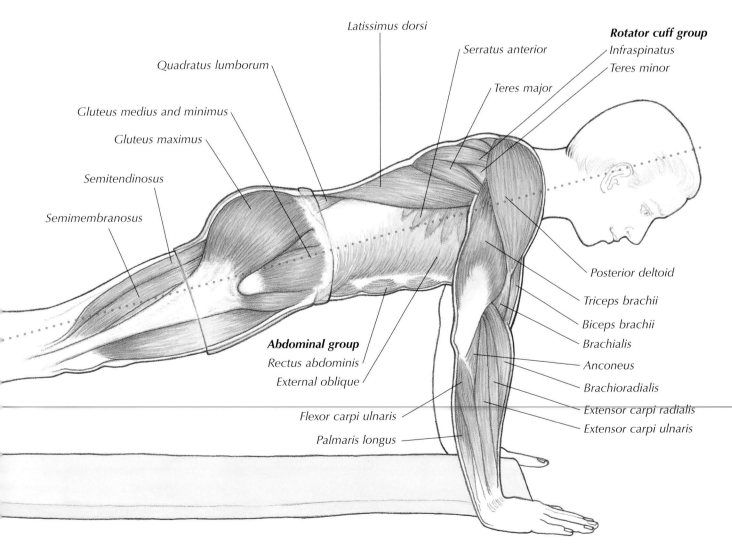

Latissimus dorsi

Serratus anterior

Rotator cuff group
Infraspinatus
Teres minor

Quadratus lumborum

Teres major

Gluteus medius and minimus

Gluteus maximus

Semitendinosus

Semimembranosus

Posterior deltoid

Triceps brachii

Biceps brachii

Brachialis

Abdominal group
Rectus abdominis
External oblique

Anconeus

Brachioradialis

Extensor carpi radialis

Extensor carpi ulnaris

Flexor carpi ulnaris

Palmaris longus

INCLINE BARBELL BENCH PRESS

Core exercise • Compound/multi-joint
• Push • Open chain • Barbell
• Intermediate to advanced

➡ The incline angle of this exercise shifts the work toward the upper chest. However most gym incline benches are usually set too high, at an angle of ±45°–60°. The ideal is more like 15°–35° from the horizontal.

Tips for good form
- Get good form before increasing weight.
- Avoid momentum; use slow, controlled motion.
- Avoid hunching the shoulders. Keep chest open and shoulder blades depressed.
- Breathe out when raising the bar.
- Keep feet wide for better stability.

Basic description
Dismount the bar from the rack. Bend elbows, lower the bar to the upper chest. Return by pressing until arms are extended. Repeat.

Pectoralis major

Brachioradialis

Biceps brachii

Brachialis

Triceps brachii

Corocobrachialis

Teres major

Latissimus dorsi

Serratus anterior

Abdominal group
External oblique
Rectus abdominis

⬅ STARTING POSITION
- Lying supine on the incline bench.
- Medium grip on bar, slightly wider than shoulder-width.
- Position body so that bar will be lowered to upper chest.
- Spine aligned (feet raised onto bench if appropriate).

Stabilizing muscles

Shoulder blades: Serratus anterior, Pectoralis minor, Rhomboids, lower Trapezius
Shoulder joint: Rotator cuff muscles, Biceps brachii
Mild trunk stabilization: Abdominal and Gluteal group, Latissimus dorsi

ANALYSIS OF MOVEMENT	JOINT 1	JOINT 2	JOINT 3
Joints	Elbow	Shoulder	Scapulothoracic
Joint movement	Up—extension Down—flexion	Up—horizontal adduction and flexion Down—horizontal abduction and flexion	Up—upward rotation, abduction Down—downward rotation, adduction
Mobilizing muscles	Triceps brachii Anconeus	Pectoralis major, emphasis on the clavicular aspect; Coracobrachialis; Anterior deltoid	Serratus anterior

ANATOMY FOR STRENGTH AND FITNESS TRAINING

DECLINE BARBELL BENCH PRESS

Core exercise • Compound/multi-joint
• Push • Open chain • Barbell
• Advanced

➡ For this exercise, you need a purpose-built decline bench. It might take some time to get used to the rush of blood to the head. To minimize dizziness, breathe steadily, and avoid holding your breath. Rise slowly after completing the exercise.

Basic description
Dismount the bar from the rack, in line with the upper chest. Bending the elbows, lower the bar in line with the upper chest. Return by pressing until the arms are extended.

STARTING POSITION
· Lying supine at a decline of ±20°–40°.
· Body stable, feet secured.
· Medium grip or wider for stability.
· Body positioned so that bar will be lowered to lower chest.

⬇

Extensor digitorum
Extensor carpi radialis brevis
Extensor carpi radialis longus
Extensor carpi ulnaris
Brachioradialis
Biceps brachii
Brachialis
Triceps brachii
Anterior deltoid
Pectoralis major

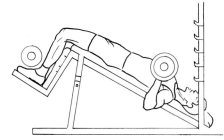

Tips for good form
· Get good form before increasing weight.
· Avoid momentum; use slow, controlled motion.
· Breathe out when raising the bar.
· Keep elbows out, in line with upper chest.

Stabilizing muscles

Shoulder blades: Serratus anterior, Rhomboids, Trapezius
Shoulder joint: Rotator cuff muscles, Biceps brachii (short head)
Mild trunk stabilization: Abdominal and Gluteal group, Latissimus dorsi

ANALYSIS OF MOVEMENT	JOINT 1	JOINT 2
Joints	Elbow	Shoulder
Joint movement	Up—extension Down—flexion	Up—combination of horizontal adduction and minor flexion
		Down—combination of horizontal abduction and minor extension
Mobilizing muscles	Triceps brachii Anconeus	Pectoralis major, emphasis on the abdominal aspect (lower) Coracobrachialis Anterior deltoid

DUMB-BELL BENCH PRESS

Core exercise • Compound/multi-joint
• Push • Open chain
Dumb-bell • Beginner to advanced

➡ A greater range of motion is possible here than in the Barbell Bench Press (see p26), allowing you to work your muscles through a greater range of motion. More stabilization is needed, as the weights need to be controlled independently.

Basic description

Bending the elbows, lower the dumb-bells in line with the upper chest. Return by pressing until the arms are extended. Repeat.

Tips for good form

· Get good form before increasing weight.
· Avoid momentum; use slow, controlled motion.
· On the up motion, do not bring dumb-bells together completely; keep them ±6 in (15cm) apart.
· Breathe out when raising the dumb-bells.

Extensor carpi radialis brevis

Extensor carpi radialis longus

Biceps brachii

Brachialis

Abdominal group

Pectoralis major

Triceps brachii

Anterior deltoid

STARTING POSITION

· Lie supine with feet on bench, or shoulder-width on ground for stability. Keep spine aligned.
· Lift dumb-bells to knees, using momentum.
· Dumb-bells are at upper chest level, supported vertically above elbows.

Stabilizing muscles

Shoulder blades: Serratus anterior, Pectoralis minor Rhomboids, lower Trapezius
Shoulder joint: Rotator cuff muscles, Biceps brachii
Mild trunk stabilization: Abdominal and Gluteal group, Latissimus dorsi

ANALYSIS OF MOVEMENT	JOINT 1	JOINT 2	JOINT 3
Joints	Elbow	Shoulder	Scapulothoracic
Joint movement	Up— extension Down—flexion	Up—horizontal adduction, flexion Down—horizontal abduction, extension	Up—partial upward rotation, abduction Down—partial downward rotation, adduction
Mobilizing muscles	Triceps brachii	Pectoralis major, emphasis on the sternal and clavicular aspect Coracobrachialis Anterior deltoid	Serratus anterior

ANATOMY FOR STRENGTH AND FITNESS TRAINING

PEC DECK MACHINE

Auxiliary exercise • Isolated/single joint
• Push • Open chain • Machine
• Beginner to advanced

This machine goes by a variety of names, including Butterfly machine and Chest Fly machine.

Basic description

Push the pads together in front of the chest, and control them back to the side. Repeat.

Tips for good form

· Get good form before increasing weight.
· Sit tall, spine aligned, on sitting bones.
· Avoid momentum; use slow, controlled motion.
· Avoid hunching or rounding shoulders during exercise. Keep the chest open and shoulder blades depressed.
· Breathe in when squeezing pads together.
· Keep feet wide for better stability.

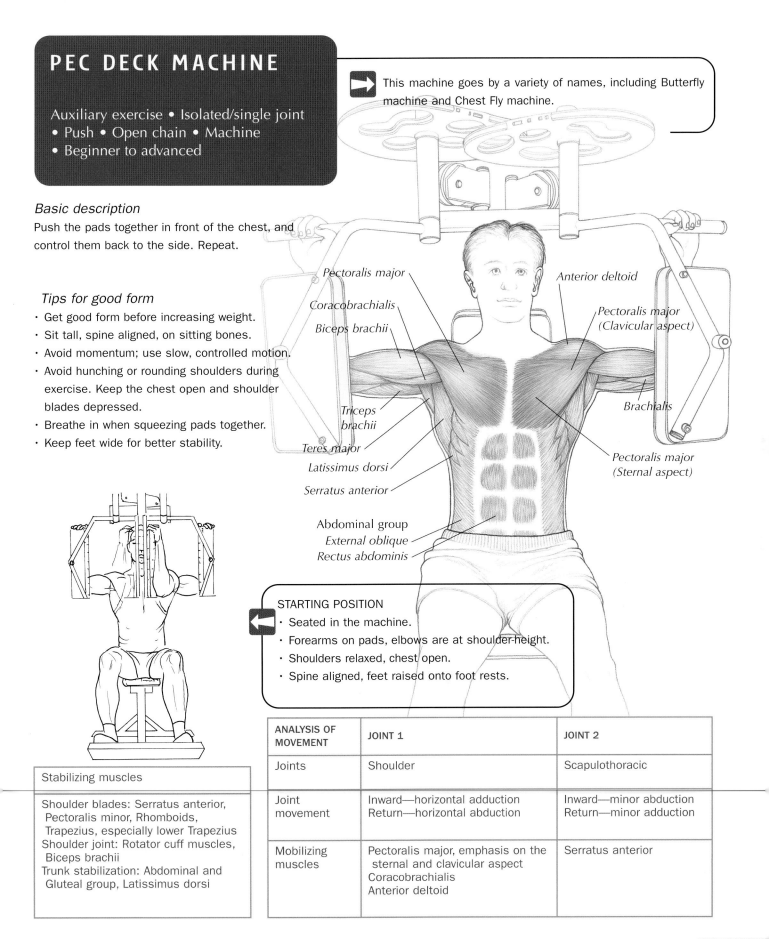

Pectoralis major
Coracobrachialis
Biceps brachii
Triceps brachii
Teres major
Latissimus dorsi
Serratus anterior
Abdominal group
External oblique
Rectus abdominis

Anterior deltoid
Pectoralis major (Clavicular aspect)
Brachialis
Pectoralis major (Sternal aspect)

STARTING POSITION

· Seated in the machine.
· Forearms on pads, elbows are at shoulder height.
· Shoulders relaxed, chest open.
· Spine aligned, feet raised onto foot rests.

Stabilizing muscles

Shoulder blades: Serratus anterior, Pectoralis minor, Rhomboids, Trapezius, especially lower Trapezius
Shoulder joint: Rotator cuff muscles, Biceps brachii
Trunk stabilization: Abdominal and Gluteal group, Latissimus dorsi

ANALYSIS OF MOVEMENT	JOINT 1	JOINT 2
Joints	Shoulder	Scapulothoracic
Joint movement	Inward—horizontal adduction Return—horizontal abduction	Inward—minor abduction Return—minor adduction
Mobilizing muscles	Pectoralis major, emphasis on the sternal and clavicular aspect Coracobrachialis Anterior deltoid	Serratus anterior

DUMB-BELL FLAT BENCH FLYES

Auxiliary exercise • Isolation/single joint
• Push • Open chain • Dumb-bell
• Beginner to advanced

→ This exercise requires good stabilization and alignment at the shoulder and scapulothoracic regions.

Basic description
Lower dumb-bells to sides until chest muscles are stretched. Return and repeat.

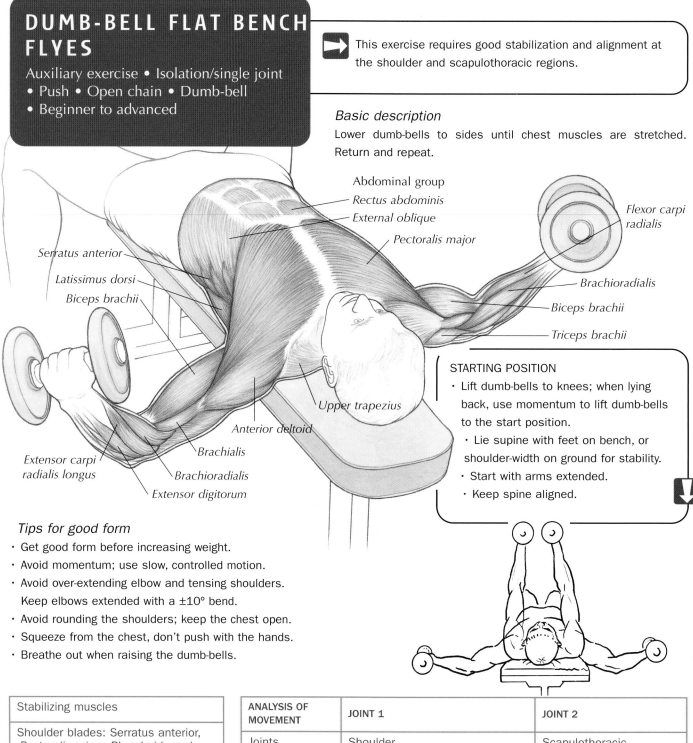

STARTING POSITION
· Lift dumb-bells to knees; when lying back, use momentum to lift dumb-bells to the start position.
· Lie supine with feet on bench, or shoulder-width on ground for stability.
· Start with arms extended.
· Keep spine aligned.

Tips for good form
· Get good form before increasing weight.
· Avoid momentum; use slow, controlled motion.
· Avoid over-extending elbow and tensing shoulders. Keep elbows extended with a ±10° bend.
· Avoid rounding the shoulders; keep the chest open.
· Squeeze from the chest, don't push with the hands.
· Breathe out when raising the dumb-bells.

Stabilizing muscles
Shoulder blades: Serratus anterior, Pectoralis minor, Rhomboids and lower Trapezius Shoulder joint: Rotator cuff muscles, Biceps brachii Elbow: Triceps brachii, Brachialis Wrist: Wrist flexors Mild trunk stabilization: Abdominal and Gluteal group, Latissimus dorsi

ANALYSIS OF MOVEMENT	JOINT 1	JOINT 2
Joints	Shoulder	Scapulothoracic
Joint movement	Up—horizontal adduction Down—horizontal abduction	Inward—minor abduction Return—minor adduction
Mobilizing muscles	Pectoralis major, emphasis on the sternal and clavicular aspect Coracobrachialis, Anterior deltoid Biceps brachii (short head)	Serratus anterior

BODY-WEIGHT DIPS

Core exercise • Compound/multi-joint
• Push • Open chain Body-weight
• Intermediate to advanced

This is one of the most common and versatile exercises. Postural compensation and cheating in technique is common though. For best results, start with only as many repetitions as you can do using proper technique.

Tips for good form

· Avoid momentum; use slow controlled motion.
· Avoid hunching and rounding the shoulders, keep chest open, and shoulder blades depressed.
· Concentrate on squeezing from the chest and triceps.
· Breathe out on upward motion.

STARTING POSITION

· Mount a parallel dip bar apparatus.
· Support your body-weight with extended arms, keep your chest open and lean slightly forward from the trunk.

Basic description

Lower body until chest is slightly stretched. Control your movement with arm strength. Push body up in same posture and repeat.

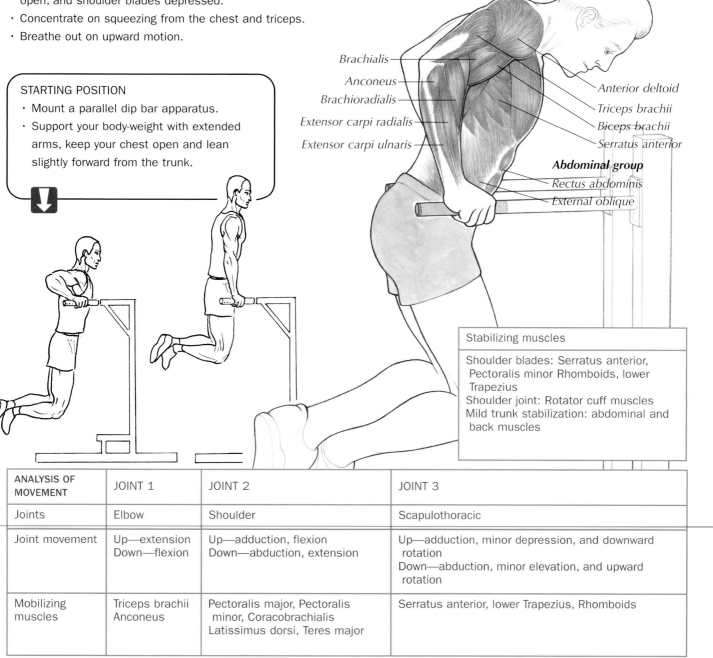

Brachialis
Anconeus
Brachioradialis
Extensor carpi radialis
Extensor carpi ulnaris
Anterior deltoid
Triceps brachii
Biceps brachii
Serratus anterior
Abdominal group
Rectus abdominis
External oblique

Stabilizing muscles

Shoulder blades: Serratus anterior, Pectoralis minor Rhomboids, lower Trapezius
Shoulder joint: Rotator cuff muscles
Mild trunk stabilization: abdominal and back muscles

ANALYSIS OF MOVEMENT	JOINT 1	JOINT 2	JOINT 3
Joints	Elbow	Shoulder	Scapulothoracic
Joint movement	Up—extension Down—flexion	Up—adduction, flexion Down—abduction, extension	Up—adduction, minor depression, and downward rotation Down—abduction, minor elevation, and upward rotation
Mobilizing muscles	Triceps brachii Anconeus	Pectoralis major, Pectoralis minor, Coracobrachialis Latissimus dorsi, Teres major	Serratus anterior, lower Trapezius, Rhomboids

CABLE CROSSOVER

Auxiliary exercise • Isolation/single joint • Push • Open chain • Cable machine • Intermediate to advanced

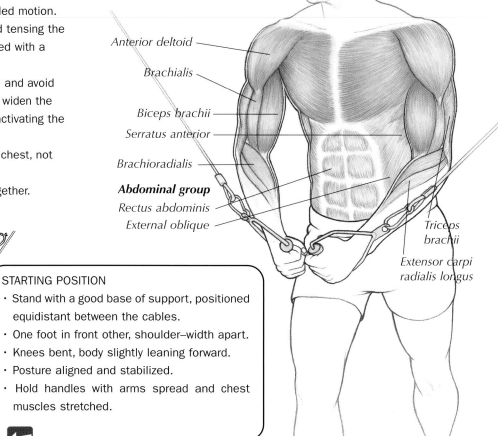

The Cable Crossover is done on a bilateral cable-pulley machine. In the 1950s, US fitness pioneer Jack LaLanne developed the first commercial gym cable-pulley machine.

Basic description

Bring cable attachments together in front. Keep elbows in a fixed position. Return to starting position and repeat. Rotate shoulders inward on the forward motion, rotate outward on return.

Anterior deltoid

Brachialis

Biceps brachii

Serratus anterior

Brachioradialis

Abdominal group
Rectus abdominis
External oblique

Triceps brachii

Extensor carpi radialis longus

Tips for good form

· Get good form before increasing weight.
· Avoid momentum; use slow, controlled motion.
· Avoid over-extending the elbows and tensing the shoulders. Keep the elbows extended with a ±10° bend.
· Keep the chest and shoulders open and avoid rounding them. Aim to depress and widen the shoulder blades against the back, activating the Serratus anterior.
· Concentrate on squeezing from the chest, not pushing with the hands.
· Exhale when bringing the cables together.

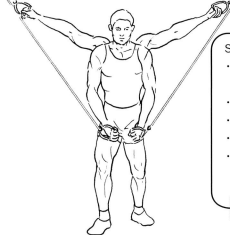

STARTING POSITION
· Stand with a good base of support, positioned equidistant between the cables.
· One foot in front other, shoulder–width apart.
· Knees bent, body slightly leaning forward.
· Posture aligned and stabilized.
· Hold handles with arms spread and chest muscles stretched.

Stabilizing muscles
Shoulder blades: Serratus anterior, Pectoralis minor, Rhomboids, lower Trapezius Shoulder joint: Rotator cuff muscles, Biceps brachii Elbow: Triceps brachii, Brachialis Wrist: Wrist flexors Mild trunk stabilization: Abdominal and Gluteal group, Latissimus dorsi General leg muscles maintain the standing position

ANALYSIS OF MOVEMENT	JOINT 1	JOINT 2
Joints	Shoulder	Scapulothoracic
Joint movement	Forward—horizontal adduction, internal rotation Return—horizontal abduction, external rotation	Forward—abduction Return—adduction
Mobilizing muscles	Pectoralis major, emphasis on the sternal and clavicular aspect Pectoralis minor; Anterior deltoid Coracobrachialis; Biceps brachii (short head); Latissimus dorsi	Serratus anterior

ANATOMY FOR STRENGTH AND FITNESS TRAINING

STRETCH BAND CHEST PRESS

Auxiliary exercise • Compound/multi-joint • Push • Open chain • Accessory • Beginner to intermediate

➡ Exercise bands were originally used in physical therapy, but with the expansion of home training, they became a useful option in strength training routines.

Tips for good form

- Slow, controlled movement, avoid momentum.
- Maintain alignment.
- Avoid hunching or rounding the shoulders. Keep the chest open. Aim to depress and widen the shoulder blades against the back, activating the Serratus anterior.
- Exhale on forward movement.

STARTING POSITION

- Standing, feet shoulder-width apart.
- Keep knees soft, not locked.
- Posture aligned and stabilized.

Basic description

Grasp the ends of the stretch band and place it behind your back, under the arms at chest level. Lift and bend your elbows to chest level. Keep the wrists firm and palms parallel to the floor. Extend your arms straight in front of the body. Return and repeat.

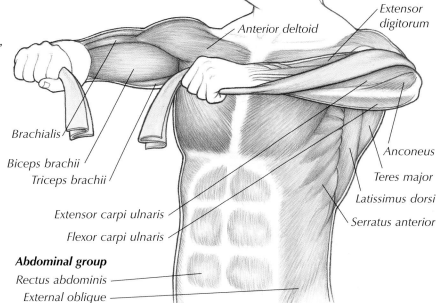

Anterior deltoid

Extensor digitorum

Brachialis

Biceps brachii

Triceps brachii

Anconeus

Teres major

Latissimus dorsi

Serratus anterior

Extensor carpi ulnaris

Flexor carpi ulnaris

Abdominal group

Rectus abdominis

External oblique

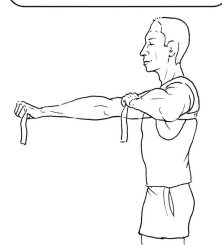

Stabilizing muscles	Although this is a seemingly simple exercise, there is significant stabilization emphasis: Shoulder blades: Serratus anterior, Pectoralis minor, Rhomboids, lower Trapezius Shoulder joint: Rotator cuff muscles, Biceps brachii Trunk stabilization: Abdominal and Gluteal group, Quadratus lumborum, and all leg muscles

ANALYSIS OF MOVEMENT	JOINT 1	JOINT 2	JOINT 3
Joints	Elbow	Shoulder	Scapulothoracic
Joint movement	Forward—extension Return—flexion	Forward—horizontal adduction Return—horizontal abduction	Forward—partial upward rotation, abduction Return—partial downward rotation, adduction
Mobilizing muscles	Triceps brachii Anconeus	Pectoralis major, emphasis on the sternal and clavicular aspects Coracobrachialis, Anterior deltoid	Serratus anterior

LEGS AND HIPS

Major muscles of the legs and hips

Name	Joints crossed	Origin	Insertion	Action
Gastrocnemius	Ankle and knee	Condyles at the base of the femur	Posterior surface of the calcaneus at the back of the heel	Ankle plantarflexion (strong); Knee flexion (weak)
Soleus	Ankle	Upper two-thirds of the posterior surface of tibia and fibula	Posterior surface of the calcaneus, at back of heel	Ankle plantarflexion
Quadriceps: Rectus femoris	Hip and knee	Anterior, inferior iliac spine of the pelvis	Patella (knee cap) and the patella ligament to the tibial tuberosity	Hip flexion Knee extension
Quadriceps: Vastii: **Vastus lateralis** **Vastus intermedius** **Vastus medialis**	Knee	Lateral, anterior, and medial surface of the femur	Into the patella border	Knee extension
Hamstrings: Short and long biceps femoris (lateral aspect); Semitendinosus and Semimembranosus (medial aspect). (Generally work as one muscle)	Hip and knee	Bicep femoris—short head on the posterior femur, on the lower Linea aspera, and the Lateral condyloid ridge. The other heads originate on the Ischial tuberosity of the pelvis	Biceps femoris inserts onto the head of the fibula and the Lateral condyle of the tibia. Semitendinosus/Semi-membranosus inserts onto medial condyle of the tibia	Hip: Extension Knee: Flexion Biceps femoris also actions lateral rotation of the hip and knee. Semitendinosus/Semi-membranosus medially rotate the hip and knee
Adductor group: Pectineus, Adductor brevis, Adductor longus, Adductor magnus, Gracilis (Generally act as one muscle)	Hip (Gracilis also crosses the knee)	Pubis and ischium of the pelvis	Along the medial femur, on the lesser trochanter, linea aspera, and medial condyloid ridge. The Gracilis inserts on the medial superior tibia	Main action is hip adduction
Tensor fasciae latae	Hip	Anterior superior iliac spine	Iliotibial band (ITB)	Hip: abduction, flexion assists medial rotation
Gluteus maximus	Hip	Posterior crest of the ilium, sacrum, and fascia of the lumbar vertebrae	Iliotibial band of the fasciae latae	Hip: extension, lateral rotation
Gluteus medius and minimus (together known as abductors)	Hip	Outer surface of the ilium (both)	Greater trochanter of the femur (both)	Hip: Abduction, lateral rotation (medius), medial rotation (medius, minimus)
Iliopsoas	Hip	Inner surface of the ilium, base of the sacrum, sides of last thoracic, and five lumbar vertebrae	Lesser trochanter of the femur	Hip flexion

ANATOMY FOR STRENGTH AND FITNESS TRAINING

Deep lateral rotators of the hip: Piriformis, Gemellus superior and inferior, Obturator externus and internus, Quadratus femoris (Found deep to the gluteus maximus)	Hip	Anterior sacrum, the posterior ischium, and the obturator foramen	Superior and inferior aspects of the greater trochanter	Hip lateral rotation

Leg muscles

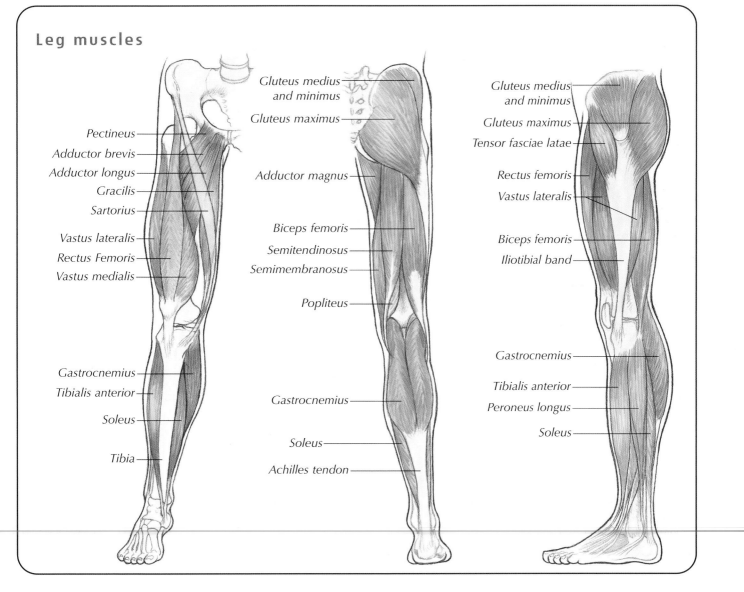

Gluteus medius and minimus
Gluteus maximus

Pectineus
Adductor brevis
Adductor longus
Gracilis
Sartorius
Vastus lateralis
Rectus Femoris
Vastus medialis

Gastrocnemius
Tibialis anterior
Soleus
Tibia

Adductor magnus

Biceps femoris
Semitendinosus
Semimembranosus

Popliteus

Gastrocnemius

Soleus
Achilles tendon

Gluteus medius and minimus
Gluteus maximus
Tensor fasciae latae

Rectus femoris
Vastus lateralis

Biceps femoris
Iliotibial band

Gastrocnemius

Tibialis anterior
Peroneus longus

Soleus

Notes:

Other significant leg muscles, not detailed here for purposes of simplicity, include the Tibialis (both anterior and posterior), the Peroneals, and the Sartorius.

BARBELL SQUAT

Core exercise • Compound/multi-joint
• Push • Closed chain • Barbell
• Intermediate to advanced

The Barbell Squat has broad value and application in training, from heavy-duty body-building, to functional training and back rehabilitation. The stresses placed on the joints and muscles during closed chain movements are more functional and offer more natural stresses on the body when compared with open chain exercises, such as leg extensions (see p56).

Basic description

Slowly lower the body, moving the hips back as if sitting on a chair. Lower to approximately 90° of knee flexion, i.e. stop before the upper leg becomes parallel with the floor. Return and repeat.

Tips for good form

· Get good form before increasing weight.
· Avoid momentum; use slow, controlled movements.
· Keep posture aligned and the spine neutral.
· Chest open, avoid rounding the shoulders.
· Keep the knees from passing over the vertical line of the toes.
· Keep your weight directly over the heel to mid-foot. Avoid lifting the heels.
· If lumbar curvature cannot be maintained, lower to less than 90°. Start with as little as 45° movement at knee.
· Inhaling on the downward phase helps to increase intra-abdominal pressure, which keeps the shoulders open, and prevents spinal flexion. Exhale on upward movement.

STARTING POSITION
· Take the bar off the squat rack and move back into a safe space for squatting.
· Stand, feet shoulder-width apart, with soft knees.
· Hold bar wider than shoulders, as is comfortable.

ANALYSIS OF MOVEMENT	JOINT 1	JOINT 2
Joints	Hip	Knee
Joint movement	Down—flexion Up—extension	Down—flexion Up—extension
Mobilizing muscles	Gluteus maximus Hamstring group	Quadricep group

Stabilizing muscles
Trunk: Abdominal group, Erector spinae, Quadratus lumborum
Hips: Gluteus medius and minimus, Deep lateral rotators, Adductor group
Lower leg: Ankle stabilizers, Gastrocnemius

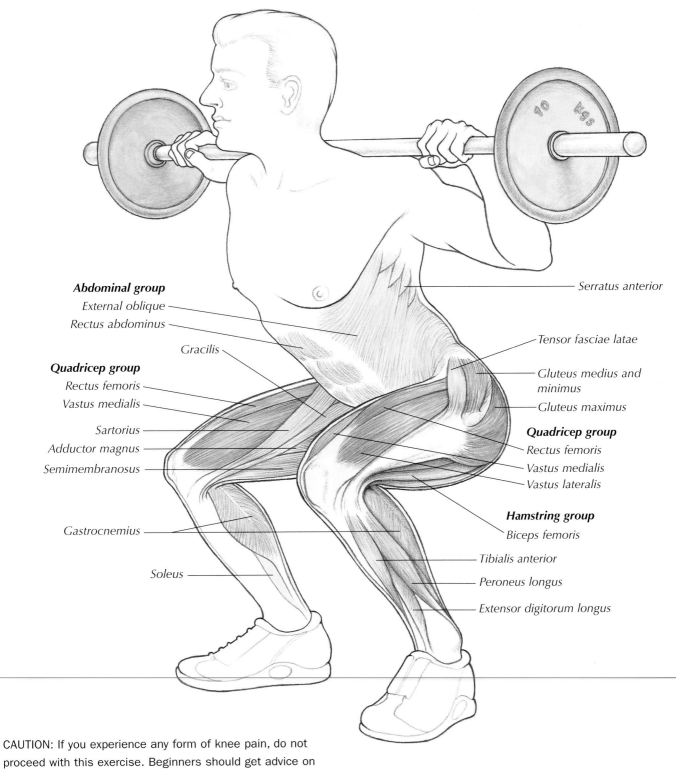

Abdominal group
External oblique
Rectus abdominus

Gracilis

Quadricep group
Rectus femoris
Vastus medialis

Sartorius
Adductor magnus
Semimembranosus

Gastrocnemius

Soleus

Serratus anterior

Tensor fasciae latae

Gluteus medius and minimus

Gluteus maximus

Quadricep group
Rectus femoris
Vastus medialis
Vastus lateralis

Hamstring group
Biceps femoris

Tibialis anterior
Peroneus longus
Extensor digitorum longus

CAUTION: If you experience any form of knee pain, do not proceed with this exercise. Beginners should get advice on what weight to start with.

FREE-STANDING SQUAT

Core exercise • Compound/multi-joint
• Push • Closed chain • Body-weight
• Beginner to Intermediate

The Squat is one of the most basic core movements. This page focuses on the mechanical basics of posture and alignment. It is essential that these are correct before proceeding to any leg exercises.

Tips for good form

· Keep posture aligned and the spine neutral.
· Chest open, avoid rounding the shoulders.
· Keep the knees from passing over the vertical line of the toes.
· Weight directly over the heel to mid-foot. Avoid lifting the heels.
· If lumbar curvature cannot be maintained, lower less than 90° at the knee. Start with 45° flexion.
· Inhale on the downward phase, exhale up.

ANALYSIS OF MOVEMENT	JOINT 1	JOINT 2
Joints	Hip	Knee
Joint movement	Down—flexion Up—extension	Down—flexion Up—extension
Mobilizing muscles	Gluteus maximus Hamstring group	Quadricep group

Stabilizing muscles	Trunk: Abdominal group, Erector spinae, Quadratus lumborum Hips: Gluteus medius and minimus, Deep lateral rotators, Adductor group

Basic description

Slowly lower the body, moving the hips back as if sitting into a chair. Lower to approximately 90° of knee flexion, i.e. stop before the upper leg becomes parallel with the floor. Return and repeat.

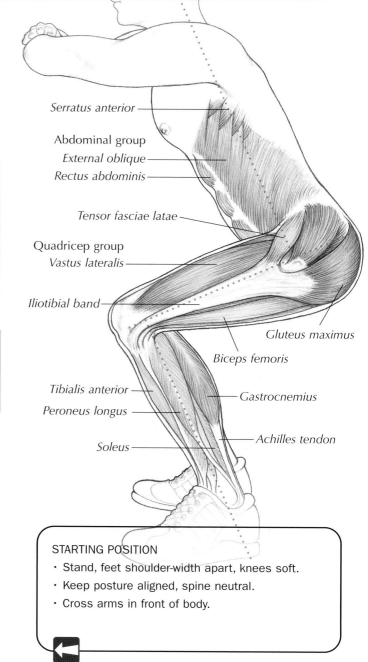

Serratus anterior

Abdominal group
External oblique
Rectus abdominis

Tensor fasciae latae

Quadricep group
Vastus lateralis

Iliotibial band

Gluteus maximus

Biceps femoris

Tibialis anterior
Peroneus longus

Gastrocnemius

Soleus

Achilles tendon

STARTING POSITION
· Stand, feet shoulder-width apart, knees soft.
· Keep posture aligned, spine neutral.
· Cross arms in front of body.

ANATOMY FOR STRENGTH AND FITNESS TRAINING

BARBELL PLIÉ SQUAT

Core exercise • Compound/multi-joint •
Push • Closed chain • Barbell
• Intermediate to advanced

➡ There are countless variations of the squat exercise. The Plié Squat, which takes it name from the French term meaning "bent," refers to the ballet movement of knee bends done with the legs turned out.

Basic description

Slowly lower the body, moving the hips back as if sitting into a chair. Lower to approximately 90° of knee flexion, i.e. stop before the upper leg becomes parallel with the floor. Return and repeat.

Tips for good form

· Get good form before increasing weight.
· Avoid momentum; use slow, controlled movement.
· Keep posture aligned and spine neutral.
· Chest open, avoid rounding the shoulders.
· Keep the knees from passing over the vertical line of the toes and prevent knees and ankles from rolling inward.
· Keep weight directly over the heel to mid-foot. Avoid lifting the heels.
· Inhale on the downward phase; exhale on upward movement.

Quadricep group
Rectus femoris
Vastus medius
Sartorius
Semitendinosus
Gracilis
Soleus

Serratus anterior
Abdominal group
External oblique
Rectus abdominis
Pectineus
Adductor longus
Semimembranosus
Gastrocnemius

STARTING POSITION

· If using the squat rack, take the bar off the rack, as described in the Barbell Squat (see p40).
· Stand with feet double shoulder-width apart and up to 45° outwardly rotated. Keep knees soft.

Stabilizing muscles

Trunk: Abdominal group, Erector spinae, Quadratus lumborum
Hips: Deep lateral rotators, Gluteus medius and minimus, Adductor group
Lower leg: Ankle stabilizers, Gastrocnemius

ANALYSIS OF MOVEMENT	JOINT 1	JOINT 2
Joints	Hip	Knee
Joint movement	Down—flexion, abduction Up—extension, adduction	Down—flexion Up—extension
Mobilizing muscles	Gluteus maximus Hamstring group Adductor group	Quadricep group (emphasis is on lateral aspects)

MACHINE INCLINE LEG PRESS

Core exercise • Compound/multi-joint
• Push • Open chain • Machine
• Intermediate to advanced

Leg press machines have been around since 1943 when Clancy Ross and Leo Stern developed the first one. The Machine Incline Leg Press is one of several different leg presses now available. It is thought to be biomechanically safer than the Vertical Leg Press machine.

Basic description

Lower the weight platform by flexing the hips and knees to approximately 90° of knee flexion. Return to the start position and repeat.

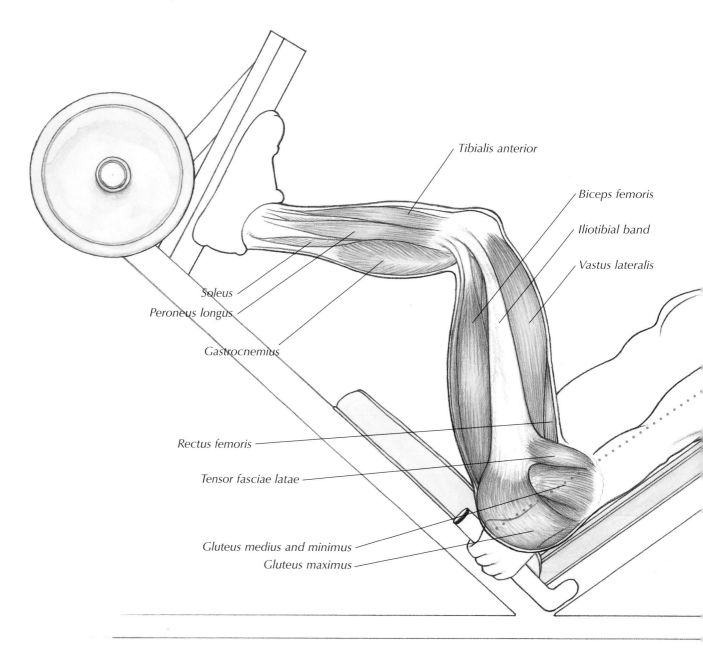

Tibialis anterior

Biceps femoris

Iliotibial band

Vastus lateralis

Soleus

Peroneus longus

Gastrocnemius

Rectus femoris

Tensor fasciae latae

Gluteus medius and minimus

Gluteus maximus

ANATOMY FOR STRENGTH AND FITNESS TRAINING

STARTING POSITION

- Sit into the machine, with your back flat against the rear seat pad.
- Place feet on platform, shoulder-width apart.
- Knees should be slightly bent, feet flat.
- Release brake lever, push its handles to the side.
- The weight will now be supported by the legs, in the ready position.
- Keep posture aligned, spine neutral.
- Keep knees soft.

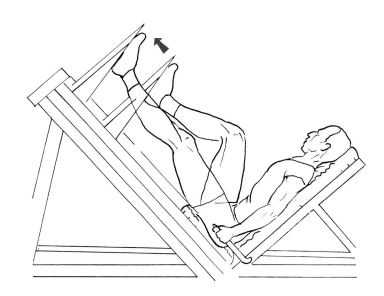

Tips for good form

- Get a proper demonstration and instruction before using this machine.
- Get good form before increasing weight.
- Avoid momentum; use slow, controlled movement.
- During movement the lower back should remain against the rear pad. The angle of the back support may need to be adjusted.
- If lumbar position cannot be maintained, lower to less than 90° knee flexion.
- Keep posture aligned and the spine neutral.
- Chest open, avoid rounding the shoulders.
- Keep the knees from passing over the vertical line of the toes.
- Keep your weight directly over the heel to mid-foot. Avoid lifting the heels. Push through the feet.
- Inhale on the downward phase; exhale on the upward movement.

Stabilizing muscles
Trunk: Abdominal group, Erector spinae, Quadratus lumborum Hips: Gluteus medius and minimus, Deep lateral rotators, Adductor group Lower leg: Ankle stabilizers, Gastrocnemius

ANALYSIS OF MOVEMENT	JOINT 1	JOINT 2
Joints	Hip	Knee
Joint movement	Down—flexion Up—extension	Down—flexion Up—extension
Mobilizing muscles	Gluteus maximus Hamstring group	Quadricep group

HACKSQUAT MACHINE

Core exercise • Compound/multi-joint • Push • Closed chain • Machine • Advanced

➡️ The Hacksquat is an advanced exercise requiring good form and stabilization. Even so, its safety is questionable due to the strong shearing forces on the knee joint.

Tips for good form

- Only use this machine as an advanced trainer.
- During movement, the lower back should remain against the rear pad.
- Keep posture aligned and the spine neutral.
- Chest open, avoid rounding the shoulders.
- Keep the knees from passing over the vertical line of the toes.
- Keep your weight directly over the heel to mid-foot. Avoid lifting the heels.
- If lumbar curvature cannot be maintained, lower to less than 90° at the knee. Start with as little as 45° flexion.
- Inhale on the downward phase. Exhale on the upward movement.

Basic description

Flexing the hips and bending the knees, slowly lower the body to about 90° of knee flexion. Return to start position and repeat.

STARTING POSITION

- Lie supine against the machine backrest.
- Feet shoulder-width apart, quite high on platform.
- Release machine brakes and take weight onto legs.
- Keep knees soft, posture aligned, and spine neutral.

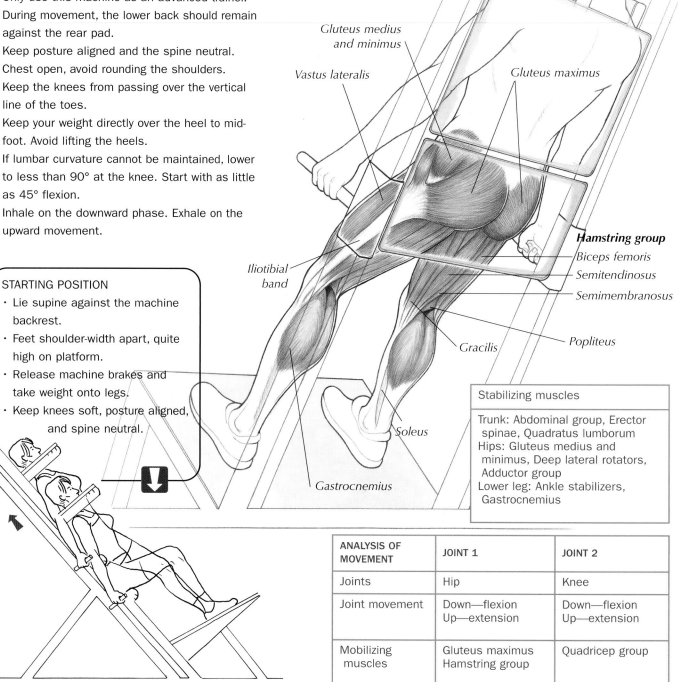

Gluteus medius and minimus

Vastus lateralis

Gluteus maximus

Iliotibial band

Hamstring group
Biceps femoris
Semitendinosus
Semimembranosus

Popliteus

Gracilis

Soleus

Gastrocnemius

Stabilizing muscles

Trunk: Abdominal group, Erector spinae, Quadratus lumborum
Hips: Gluteus medius and minimus, Deep lateral rotators, Adductor group
Lower leg: Ankle stabilizers, Gastrocnemius

ANALYSIS OF MOVEMENT	JOINT 1	JOINT 2
Joints	Hip	Knee
Joint movement	Down—flexion Up—extension	Down—flexion Up—extension
Mobilizing muscles	Gluteus maximus Hamstring group	Quadricep group

BENT LEG GOOD MORNING

- Auxiliary exercise • Isolated/single joint
- Pull • Closed chain • Barbell
- Intermediate to advanced

→ This exercise, which derives its name from its rising movement, takes you back to the classic body-building era of the 1950s and 1960s before back extension machines were built, yet its application is timeless.

Basic description

Lower the trunk by flexing at the hips until the trunk is parallel with the floor. Bend the knees slightly during the descent. Return to starting position and repeat.

Tips for good form

- Get a proper demonstration and instructions before doing this exercise.
- Good form is more important than the weight lifted. Start with a very light weight and use a smaller range of motion until you adapt.
- Maintain posture stabilization.
- Avoid rounding the back; keep it aligned.
- The less the hamstring flexibility, the more the knees will need to be bent in order to keep the back straight and maintain lumbar curvature.
- Inhale on the downward phase; exhale on the upward movement.

Gluteus maximus

Erector spinae
External obliques
Rectus abdominis
Quadratus lumborum
Gluteus medius
Tensor fasciae latae
Iliotibial band
Vastus lateralis

Hamstring group
Biceps femoris
Semitendinosus
Semimembranosus

Biceps femoris
Adductor group

Gastrocnemius

Soleus

STARTING POSITION

- Stand, feet shoulder-width apart; keep knees soft.
- Place barbell across back of shoulders (Posterior deltoid/Upper trapezius).

ANALYSIS OF MOVEMENT	JOINT 1
Joints	Hips
Joint movement	Down—flexion Up—extension
Mobilizing muscles	Gluteus maximus Hamstring group

Stabilizing muscles
Main stabilizers: Erector spinae, Quadricep group
Additional stabilization: Shoulder blades: lower and mid-Trapezius, Levator scapula, Rhomboids, Serratus anterior
Abdominal group
Hips: Gluteus medius and minimus, Deep lateral rotators, Adductor group, Quadratus lumborum
Lower leg: Ankle stabilizers, Tibialis anterior, Gastrocnemius

FREE-STANDING MODIFIED LUNGE

Core exercise • Compound/multi-joint
• Push • Closed chain • Barbell
• Beginner to advanced

A progression on the basic Squat (see p40) is the Lunge, in which you takes a step forward into a squat movement. Many variations are possible, but it is essential that the basic form is correct before proceeding to more advanced versions.

Tips for good form

· Keep the trunk upright and your weight centered between both legs during exercise.
· Avoid lifting the front heel; keep the front knee from passing over the vertical line of the toes. A common error is too much forward lean from the trunk and pressure on the front knee. Use slow, controlled movement.
· Keep the posture aligned and the spine neutral. If the hip flexors are tight, the lumbar alignment will be compromised.
· Keep the chest open, avoid rounding the shoulders.

STARTING POSITION

· Stand, feet shoulder-width apart.
· Support the bar comfortably on upper Trapezius.
· Step forward with one leg in front of other, so that the front knee is vertically above the front foot. The back leg should be far enough back so that the heel is raised.
· Bend the front leg to lower the body (see opposite).
· Keep posture aligned and spine neutral.

ANALYSIS OF MOVEMENT	JOINT 1	JOINT 2
Joints	Hip (front leg)	Knee (front leg)
Joint movement	Down—flexion Up—extension	Down—flexion Up—extension
Mobilizing muscles	Gluteus maximus Hamstring group	Quadricep group

Stabilizing muscles
Trunk: Abdominal group, Erector spinae, Quadratus lumborum Hips: Gluteus medius and minimus, Deep lateral rotators, Adductor group Lower leg: Ankle stabilizers, Gastrocnemius

Basic description

Slowly lower the body by flexing the knee and hip of the front leg, to approximately 90° of flexion. The rear knee will almost be touching the ground. Return to start position and repeat. Switch the front leg and repeat the exercise.

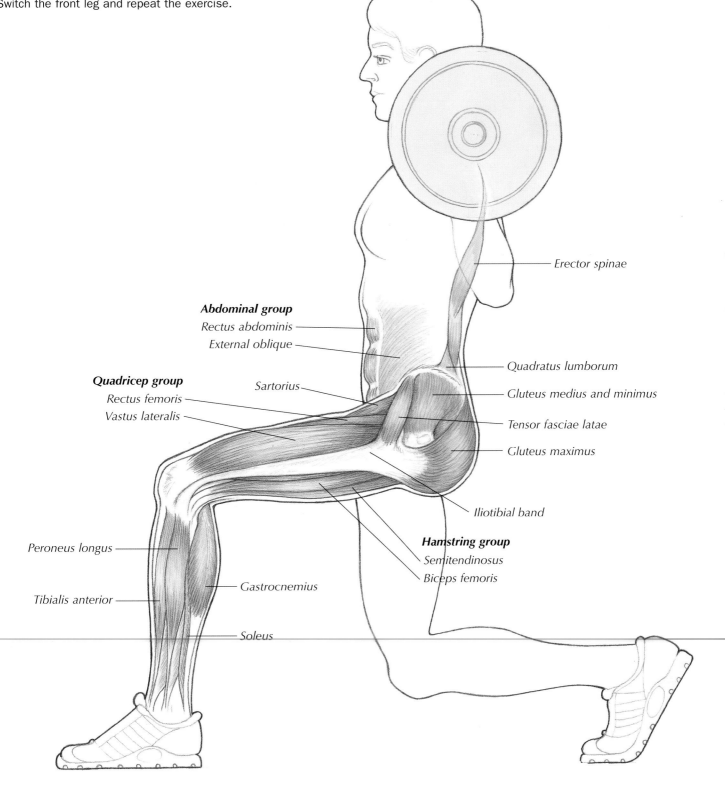

Erector spinae

Abdominal group
Rectus abdominis
External oblique

Quadratus lumborum

Gluteus medius and minimus

Quadricep group
Rectus femoris
Vastus lateralis

Sartorius

Tensor fasciae latae

Gluteus maximus

Iliotibial band

Peroneus longus

Hamstring group
Semitendinosus
Biceps femoris

Tibialis anterior

Gastrocnemius

Soleus

DOUBLE LEG BRIDGE

Auxiliary exercise • Isolated/single joint
• Push • Closed chain • Body-weight
• Beginner to advanced

Until recently, this exercise was more commonly seen in back rehabilitation and physical therapy settings. It is one of a series of core stability exercises that has slowly made its way into gym and training routines.

Basic description

Slowly raise the trunk and lower back by extending the hips. Pause, return, and repeat.

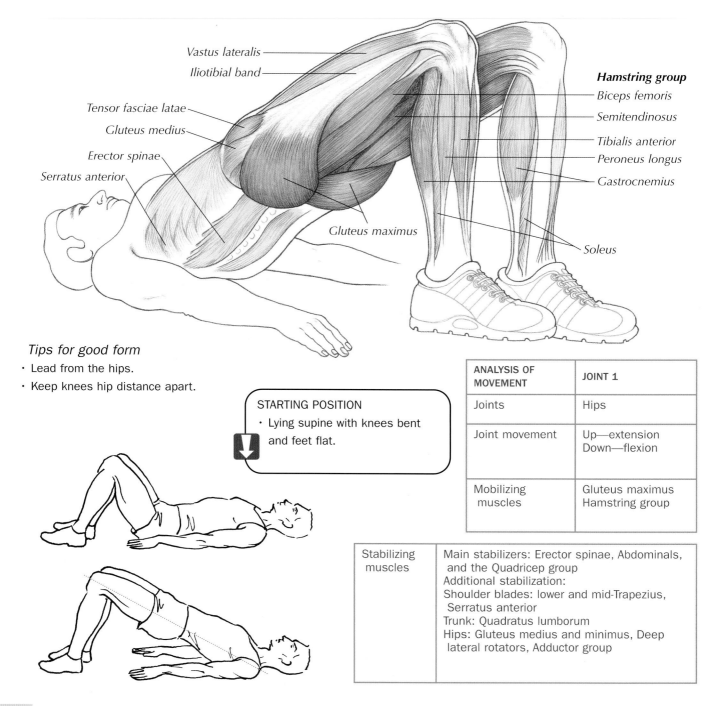

Vastus lateralis
Iliotibial band
Tensor fasciae latae
Gluteus medius
Erector spinae
Serratus anterior
Gluteus maximus

Hamstring group
Biceps femoris
Semitendinosus
Tibialis anterior
Peroneus longus
Gastrocnemius
Soleus

Tips for good form

· Lead from the hips.
· Keep knees hip distance apart.

STARTING POSITION
· Lying supine with knees bent and feet flat.

ANALYSIS OF MOVEMENT	JOINT 1
Joints	Hips
Joint movement	Up—extension Down—flexion
Mobilizing muscles	Gluteus maximus Hamstring group

Stabilizing muscles	Main stabilizers: Erector spinae, Abdominals, and the Quadricep group Additional stabilization: Shoulder blades: lower and mid-Trapezius, Serratus anterior Trunk: Quadratus lumborum Hips: Gluteus medius and minimus, Deep lateral rotators, Adductor group

CABLE HIP EXTENSIONS

Auxiliary exercise • Isolation/single joint
• Push • Open chain • Machine
• Beginner to advanced

➡ This popular gym exercise is frequently done incorrectly, with common errors including too much weight and momentum, and postural compensation. Slow, quality movements, with moderate weight, will ensure the glutes are properly activated.

Basic description
Pull the cable attachment backward by extending the hip. Pause, return, and repeat. Repeat with opposite leg.

Tips for good form
· Avoid tilting the trunk forward or arching the lower back in the motion. The Gluteus maximus can only extend the hip approximately 10°–15° past vertical. Movement beyond that is likely to come from lower back extension.
· Keep the posture aligned and stabilized.
· Work slowly and avoid momentum.

STARTING POSITION
· Attach ankle cuff accessory to low cable pulley and strap it to one leg.
· Stand on a step or other slight raise to give clearance for movement.

⬇

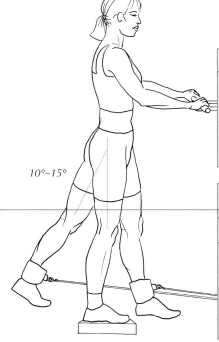

10°–15°

Erector spinae

Quadratus lumborum

Tensor fasciae latae

Gluteus medius and minimus

Gluteus maximus

Iliotibial band

Vastus lateralis

Hamstring group
Biceps femoris
Semimembranosus
Semitendinosus

Gastrocnemius

Peroneus longus

Tibialis anterior

Soleus

Stabilizing muscles

Main stabilizers: Erector spinae, Abdominal group, Gluteus medius and minimus, Quadratus lumborum
The muscles in the stationary leg are also significant stabilizers

ANALYSIS OF MOVEMENT	JOINT 1
Joints	Hip
Joint movement	Back—extension Forward—flexion
Mobilizing muscles	Gluteus maximus Hamstring group

PRONE HIP EXTENSIONS

Auxiliary exercise • Isolated/single joint
• Push • Open chain • Body-weight
• Intermediate to advanced

➡ This simple but advanced exercise places most emphasis on the ability to stabilize the trunk. People with acute lower back problems should not attempt it.

Tips for good form
· Work slowly, avoid compensating with momentum or trunk movement.
· Avoid lumbar movement.
· Keep the trunk and spine stabilized. Focus on abdominal stabilization.

Basic description
Holding the bench, keep the legs straight and extend them from the hip until legs are parallel with the floor or just beyond. Pause, return, and repeat.

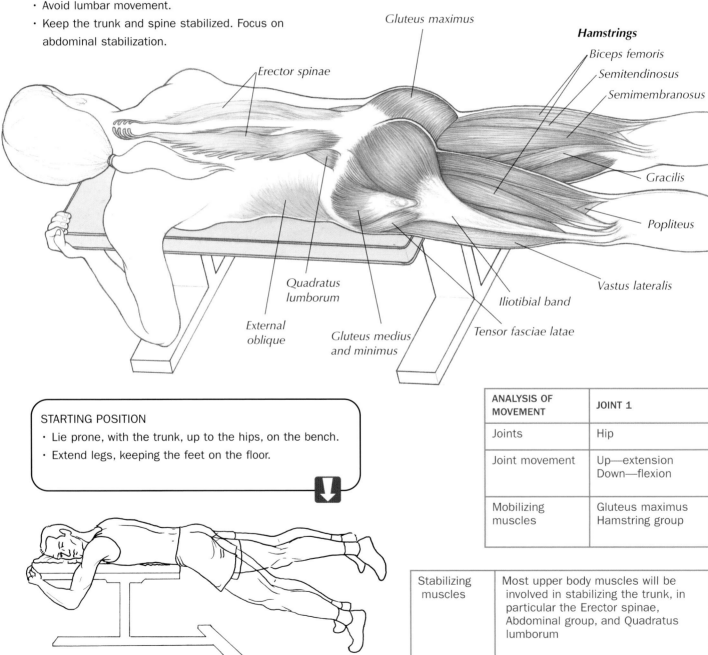

Gluteus maximus

Hamstrings
Biceps femoris
Semitendinosus
Semimembranosus
Gracilis
Popliteus
Vastus lateralis

Erector spinae

Quadratus lumborum

External oblique

Gluteus medius and minimus

Iliotibial band

Tensor fasciae latae

STARTING POSITION
· Lie prone, with the trunk, up to the hips, on the bench.
· Extend legs, keeping the feet on the floor.

⬇

ANALYSIS OF MOVEMENT	JOINT 1
Joints	Hip
Joint movement	Up—extension Down—flexion
Mobilizing muscles	Gluteus maximus Hamstring group

Stabilizing muscles	Most upper body muscles will be involved in stabilizing the trunk, in particular the Erector spinae, Abdominal group, and Quadratus lumborum

HIP ADDUCTOR MACHINE

Auxiliary exercise • Isolated/single joint • Pull • Open chain • Machine • Beginner to advanced

"Spot reduction," the concept that training an area repeatedly can shape and tone it through local weight-loss, led to the popularity of the Adductor and Abductor machines. Used correctly, these benefit the adductor's role as postural stabilizers and safeguard against medial knee injuries.

Tips for good form
· Work slowly against moderate resistance. Avoid momentum.
· Concentrate on squeezing from the adductors, as opposed to working from the feet.

Basic description
Squeeze the legs together. Pause, return, and repeat.

Abdominal group
External oblique
Rectus abdominis

Gluteus medius and minimus

Adductor group
Pectineus
Adductor longus
Adductor magnus
Gracilis
Rectus femoris
Vastus medialis
Sartorius

Gastrocnemius

Soleus

Quadricep group
Vastus medialis
Rectus femoris
Vastus lateralis

Tibialis anterior
Gastrocnemius
Peroneus longus

STARTING POSITION
· Seated in the machine, legs against the pads.
· Sit on the sitting bones, keep chest open, and spine aligned.
· Some machines need a lever release to position the legs properly.

ANALYSIS OF MOVEMENT	JOINT 1
Joints	Hip
Joint movement	Inward—adduction Outward—abduction
Mobilizing muscles	Adductor group

Stabilizing muscles
Trunk: Abdominals group, Erector spinae, Quadratus lumborum

HIP ABDUCTOR MACHINE

Auxiliary exercise • Isolation/single joint
• Push • Open chain • Machine
• Beginner to advanced

The Adductor and Abductor machines are easily confused, but the muscles they train work together as postural stabilizers (side to side). As a result, it is beneficial to train on both machines in the same session (see also p53).

Basic description
Squeeze the legs apart. Pause, return, and repeat.

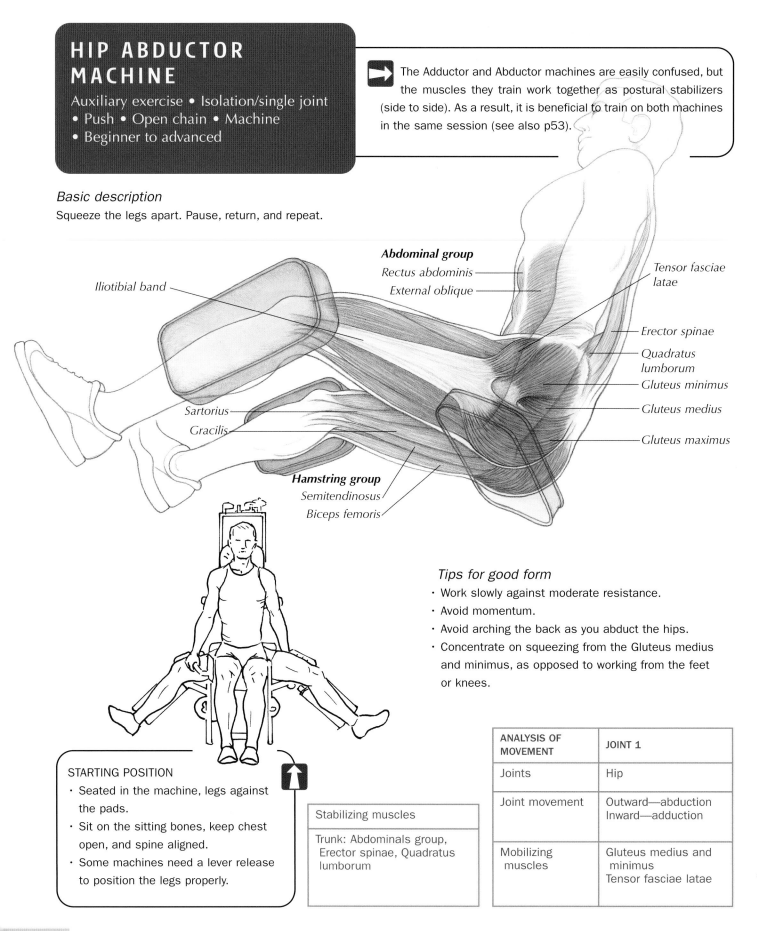

Iliotibial band

Abdominal group
Rectus abdominis
External oblique

Tensor fasciae latae

Erector spinae

Quadratus lumborum

Gluteus minimus

Gluteus medius

Gluteus maximus

Sartorius
Gracilis

Hamstring group
Semitendinosus
Biceps femoris

Tips for good form
· Work slowly against moderate resistance.
· Avoid momentum.
· Avoid arching the back as you abduct the hips.
· Concentrate on squeezing from the Gluteus medius and minimus, as opposed to working from the feet or knees.

STARTING POSITION
· Seated in the machine, legs against the pads.
· Sit on the sitting bones, keep chest open, and spine aligned.
· Some machines need a lever release to position the legs properly.

Stabilizing muscles

Trunk: Abdominals group, Erector spinae, Quadratus lumborum

ANALYSIS OF MOVEMENT	JOINT 1
Joints	Hip
Joint movement	Outward—abduction Inward—adduction
Mobilizing muscles	Gluteus medius and minimus Tensor fasciae latae

ANATOMY FOR STRENGTH AND FITNESS TRAINING

SIDE-LYING HIP ABDUCTION

Auxiliary exercise • Isolation/single joint
• Pull • Open chain • Body-weight
• Beginner to Intermediate

This exercise, probably more than any other, was popularized in the 1980s by the best-selling *Jane Fonda's Workout*. Fonda, an Oscar-winning actress, was one of the pioneers of aerobics and the home-workout video.

Basic description

Slowly side-lift the right leg through a full range of motion, by abducting the hip. Pause, slowly lower the leg, then repeat. Roll over and repeat with the other leg.

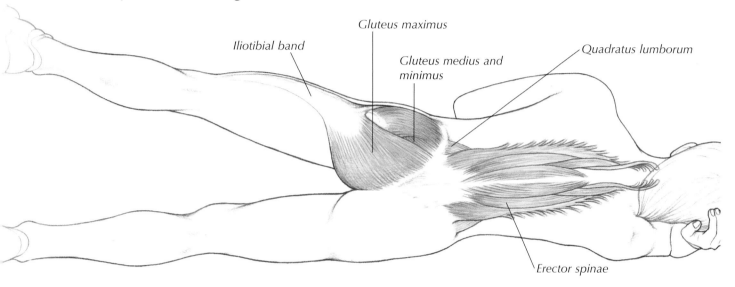

Iliotibial band

Gluteus maximus

Gluteus medius and minimus

Quadratus lumborum

Erector spinae

Tips for good form

· Avoid allowing the hips to roll forward or backward while performing the exercise; engage the abdominals to stabilize the spine and pelvis.
· Don't allow the thigh to rotate externally while lifting the leg.
· Work slowly and avoid momentum.
· Avoid over-abduction of the hip.

STARTING POSITION
· Lie on the right side with head resting on right arm.
· Keep posture aligned and underneath leg extended.

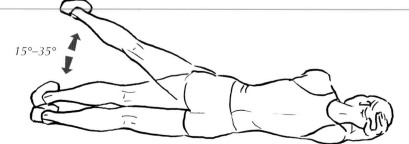

15°–35°

ANALYSIS OF MOVEMENT	JOINT 1
Joints	Hip
Joint movement	Up—abduction Down—adduction
Mobilizing muscles	Gluteus medius and minimus Tensor fasciae latae

Stabilizing muscles	Trunk: Abdominals group, Erector spinae, Quadratus lumborum

MACHINE SEATED LEG EXTENSION

Auxiliary exercise • Isolation/single joint
• Push • Open chain • Machine
• Intermediate to advanced

 Jack LaLanne, a popular fitness personality of the 1950s, is credited with inventing the Machine Seated Leg Extension, a classic isolation exercise for the Quadriceps.

Tips for good form

- Work slowly, avoid momentum.
- Avoid over-extending the knee joint, especially with momentum.
- Keep the lower back against the backrest. Avoid lifting and rocking the body.
- Focus on squeezing from the quadriceps, as opposed to lifting from the feet. Also avoid pulling on the handles to generate momentum.
- Inhale on the upward phase; exhale on downward movement.

Basic description
Lift the lower leg by extending the knees until the leg is straight. Return and repeat.

STARTING POSITION
- Sit in the machine with your back against the padded back support.
- Sit on the sitting bones, with spine aligned.
- Adjust the machine so your knee is aligned with the lever fulcrum and the padded lever is positioned on the curve of the foot.
- Hold the side handles.

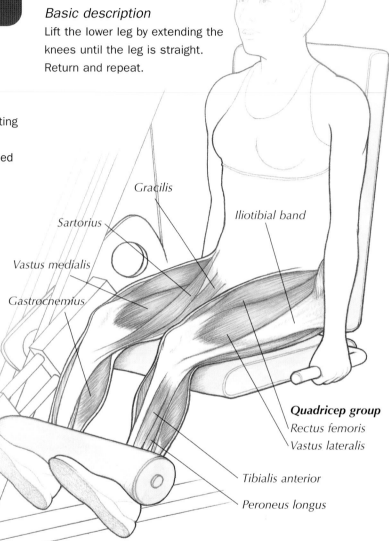

Gracilis
Iliotibial band
Sartorius
Vastus medialis
Gastrocnemius
Quadricep group
Rectus femoris
Vastus lateralis
Tibialis anterior
Peroneus longus

Stabilizing muscles
Moderate stabilization is effected by the Abdominal group, Erector spinae, lower and mid-Trapezius, Rhomboids

ANALYSIS OF MOVEMENT	JOINT 1
Joints	Knee
Joint movement	Up—extension Down—flexion
Mobilizing muscles	Quadricep group

ANATOMY FOR STRENGTH AND FITNESS TRAINING

MACHINE LYING LEG CURL

Auxiliary exercise • Isolation/single joint
• Pull • Open chain • Machine
• Intermediate to advanced

Weak hamstring muscles will pose an increased risk of knee injury during knee extension activities. The Machine Lying Leg Curl is one of the few isolation exercises for this muscle.

Basic description

Lift the lower leg by flexing the knees. Return and repeat.

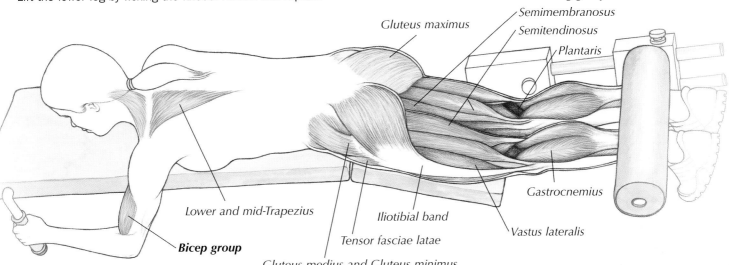

Gluteus maximus

Hamstring group
Semimembranosus
Semitendinosus
Plantaris
Gastrocnemius
Vastus lateralis

Lower and mid-Trapezius
Bicep group
Iliotibial band
Tensor fasciae latae
Gluteus medius and Gluteus minimus

Tips for good form

· Work slowly, avoid momentum.
· Avoid over-extending the knee joint or dropping the weight on the downward phase.
· Focus on abdominal stabilization to avoid lifting the hips and rocking the body and lower back.
· Squeeze from the hamstrings, as opposed to lifting from the feet. Avoid pulling on the handles to generate momentum.
· Inhale on the upward phase; exhale on downward movement.

ANALYSIS OF MOVEMENT	JOINT 1
Joints	Knees
Joint movement	Up—flexion Down—extension
Mobilizing muscles	Hamstring group Gastrocnemius

STARTING POSITION

· Lie prone on the machine, ankles tucked under the padded weight lever.
· Adjust machine so that your knees are aligned with the lever fulcrum, and the padded lever is positioned on the curve of the ankles.
· Hold onto the side handles.

Stabilizing muscles

Trunk: Abdominal group
Upper body: Bicep muscles, lower and mid-Trapezius, Serratus anterior

MACHINE STANDING CALF RAISE

Auxiliary exercise • Isolation/single joint
• Push • Closed chain • Machine
• Intermediate to advanced

➡ This is a popular calf machine exercise in the gym. However, you can do it at home by simply using the edge of a step. To increase weight, work one leg at a time.

Tips for good form

· Adjust the machine to give maximal range of movement for the calf muscle.
· Avoid bending or hyper-extending the knees.
· Increase emphasis on the calf muscle by relaxing the toes and taking them out of the effort.

STARTING POSITION

· Place toes and ball of foot on the foot platform.
· Bending the knees, and with spine aligned, step under and up into the machine, placing shoulders under the padded weight levers.
· Grasp the handles on sides of the padded levers.
· Stand up into the machine by extending hips and knees.
· Maintain postural alignment and abdominal stabilization. ⬇

Basic description
Raise the heels by plantarflexing the ankles as high as possible. Pause, then lower the heels until the calves are stretched. Repeat.

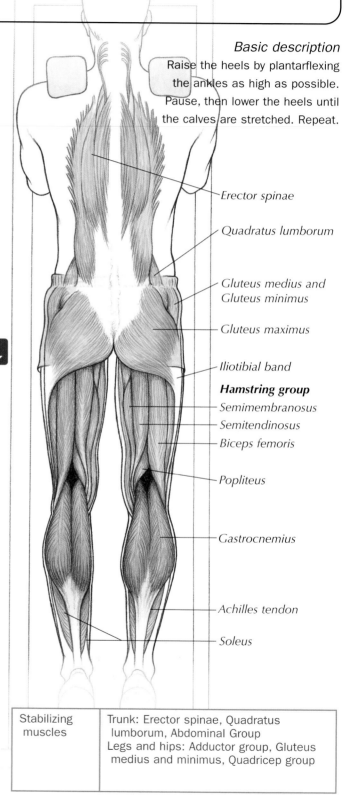

- Erector spinae
- Quadratus lumborum
- Gluteus medius and Gluteus minimus
- Gluteus maximus
- Iliotibial band
- **Hamstring group**
- Semimembranosus
- Semitendinosus
- Biceps femoris
- Popliteus
- Gastrocnemius
- Achilles tendon
- Soleus

ANALYSIS OF MOVEMENT	JOINT 1
Joints	Ankle
Joint movement	Up—plantarflexion Down—dorsiflexion
Mobilizing muscles	Emphasis is on Gastrocnemius, Soleus, Tibialis posterior, Peroneus longus

Stabilizing muscles	Trunk: Erector spinae, Quadratus lumborum, Abdominal Group Legs and hips: Adductor group, Gluteus medius and minimus, Quadricep group

MACHINE SEATED CALF RAISE

Auxiliary exercise • Isolation/singlejoint • Push • Closed chain • Machine • Intermediate to advanced

The Machine Seated Calf Raise differs from the standing version in that it places emphasis on the soleus muscle of the calf, which works best when the knee is flexed.

Basic description

Lower the heels until the calves are stretched. Raise the heels by plantarflexing the ankles as high as possible. Return to the start position and repeat.

Tips for good form

· Adjust the machine to give maximal range of movement for the calf muscle.
· Increase emphasis on the calf muscles by relaxing the toes and taking them out of the effort.

Erector spinae

Quadratus lumborum

Abdominal group
External oblique
Rectus abdominis

Gastrocnemius

Soleus

Gastrocnemius (tendon cut away)

Achilles tendon (cut away)

ANALYSIS OF MOVEMENT	JOINT 1
Joints	Ankle
Joint movement	Down—dorsiflexion Up—plantarflexion
Mobilizing muscles	Soleus muscle, Gastrocnemius, Tibialis posterior, Peroneus longus

Stabilizing muscles	Moderate stabilization from the Abdominal group, Erector spinae, lower and mid-Trapezius, and Rhomboids

STARTING POSITION

· Sit on seat, on sitting bones, spine aligned.
· Place toes and ball of foot on the foot platform.
· Place lower thighs under the weight pad, moving it onto the legs by using the machine lever. Machine should be adjusted so the weight pads offer resistance throughout full range of motion. Release support lever.
· Maintain postural alignment and abdominal stabilization.

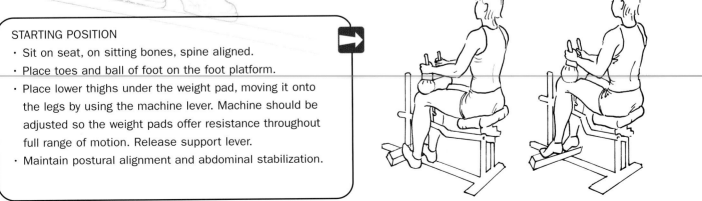

BACK AND SHOULDERS

Muscles of the back and shoulders

Name	Joints crossed	Origin	Insertion	Action
Erector spinae	Length of the spinal column	Posterior illiac crest and sacrum	Angles of ribs, transverse processes of all ribs	Spinal extension
Latissimus dorsi	Shoulder	Posterior crest of the ilium, sacrum, spineous processes of the lumbar spine, and lower six thoracic vertebrae	Medial side of the humerus	Shoulder: adduction, extension, medial rotation, horizontal abduction
Trapezius, consisting of: Upper fibres Mid fibres Lower fibres	Cross from vertebral column onto the scapula	Occipital bones, spineous processes of cervical and thoracic vertebrae	Acromion process and spine of the scapula	Together, the main action is scapular retraction. Separately: upper fibres: scapula elevation; mid fibres: scapular adduction; lower fibres: scapula depression, upward rotation
Rhomboids	Cross from vertebral column onto the scapula	Spineous process of the last cervical and the first five thoracic vertebrae	Medial border of the scapula, below the scapula spine	Scapular: retraction downward rotation
Teres major	Shoulder	Posterior, inferior lateral border of the scapula	Medial humerus	Shoulder: extension, medial rotation, adduction
Deltoids, consisting of: Posterior fibers Mid-fibers Anterior fibers	Shoulder	Posterior fibers: inferior edge of the spine of the scapula; mid fibers: lateral aspect of the acromion; anterior fibers: anterior lateral third of the clavicle	Lateral side of the humerus	Shoulder abduction. Also: Posterior fibers: shoulder extension, horizontal abduction, and lateral rotation; mid-fibers: shoulder abduction; anterior fibers: shoulder flexion, horizontal flexion, and medial rotation
Serratus anterior	Shoulder	Upper nine ribs at the side of the chest	Anterior aspect of the entire medial border of the scapula	Scapula: protraction, upward rotation
Quadratus lumborum	From the spine to the pelvis	Posterior inner surface of the iliac crest	Transverse processes of the upper four lumbar vertebrae and the lower border of the twelfth rib	Trunk lateral flexion, elevation of the pelvis (while standing)

Muscles of the rotator cuff

Name	Joints crossed	Origin	Insertion	Action
Supraspinatus	Shoulder	Supraspinious fossa	Around the greater tubercle of the humerus	Shoulder abduction (first 15°)
Infraspinatus	Shoulder	Scapular posterior surface on the medial aspect of the infraspinatus fossa, just below the scapula spine	Around the greater tubercle of the humerus	Shoulder: lateral rotation, horizontal abduction, extension
Teres minor	Shoulder	Posterior, upper and middle aspect of the lateral border of the scapula	Around the greater tubercle of the humerus	Shoulder: lateral rotation, horizontal abduction, extension
Subscapularis	Shoulder	Along the anterior surface of the subscapular fossa	Lesser tubercle of the humerus	Shoulder: medial rotation, adduction, extension

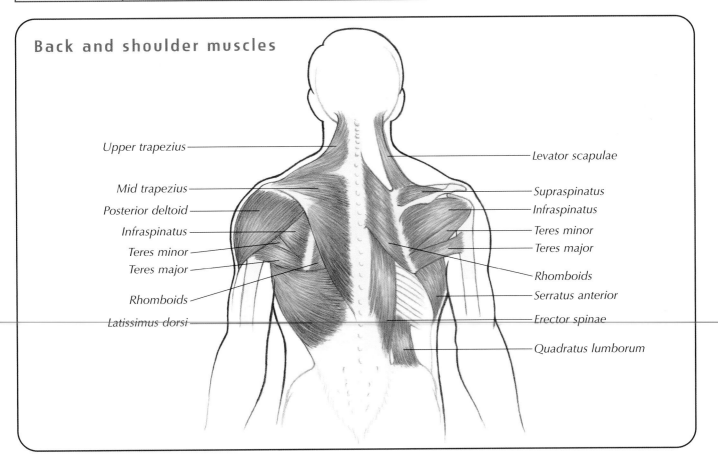

Back and shoulder muscles

Upper trapezius

Mid trapezius

Posterior deltoid

Infraspinatus

Teres minor

Teres major

Rhomboids

Latissimus dorsi

Levator scapulae

Supraspinatus

Infraspinatus

Teres minor

Teres major

Rhomboids

Serratus anterior

Erector spinae

Quadratus lumborum

MACHINE CABLE FRONT LAT PULL-DOWN

Core exercise • Compound/multi-joint
• Pull • Open chain • Machine
• Beginner to advanced

 The Lat Pull-down is one of the most complete upper body exercises, with many possible variations. The Front Lat Pull-down is more functional than its traditional counterpart to the back of the neck.

Basic description

Pull the bar down to the upper chest. Return and repeat.

Tips for good form

· Avoid momentum. Use a slow, controlled, full range of movement.
· Avoid hunching or rounding the shoulders during the exercise. Keep the chest open and shoulder blades depressed.
· Leaning slightly backward from the sitting bones will give better clearance for the bar, and activate the abdominal stabilizers.
· Inhale on the down phase.

STARTING POSITION
· Sit on the sitting bones, with the chest open and spine aligned
· Place knees under the roll pad restraint.
· Get a wide grip on the bar.
· Sit with legs underneath the machine supports.

Stabilizing muscles
Trunk: Abdominal group, Erector spinae Shoulder joint: Rotator cuff muscles Shoulder blades: Serratus anterior, Rhomboids, lower Trapezius Forearm: Wrist flexors

ANALYSIS OF MOVEMENT	JOINT 1	JOINT 2	JOINT 3
Joints	Elbow	Shoulder	Scapula
Joint movement	Down—flexion Up—extension	Down—adduction, slight extension Up—abduction, slight flexion	Down—downward rotation, adduction (retraction), depression Up—upward rotation, abduction (protraction), elevation
Mobilizing muscles	Biceps brachii Brachialis Brachoradialis	Latissimus dorsi Teres major Pectoralis major Posterior deltoid	Rhomboids, Trapezius

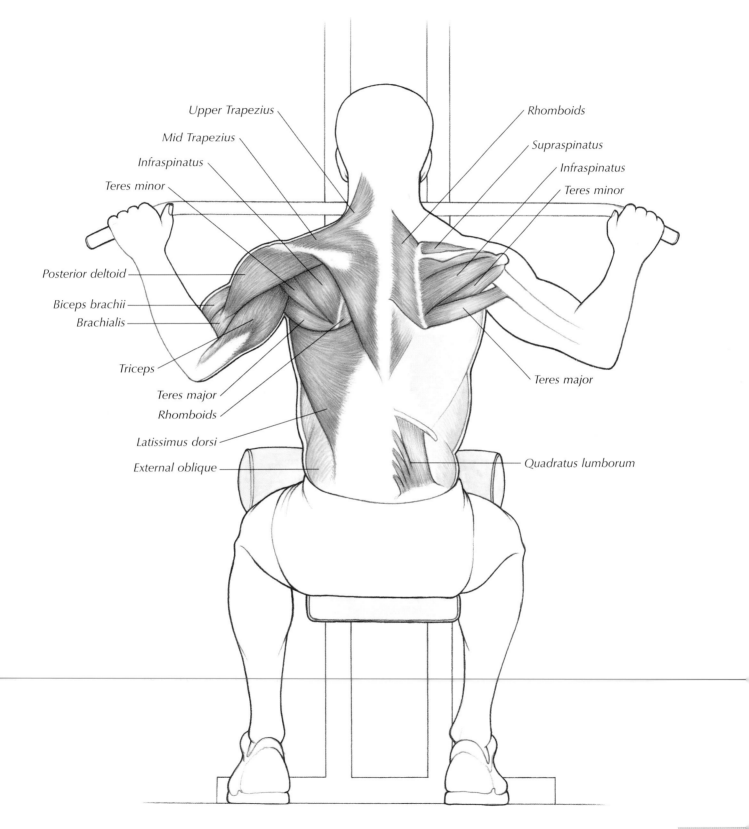

Upper Trapezius

Mid Trapezius

Infraspinatus

Teres minor

Posterior deltoid

Biceps brachii

Brachialis

Triceps

Teres major

Rhomboids

Latissimus dorsi

External oblique

Rhomboids

Supraspinatus

Infraspinatus

Teres minor

Teres major

Quadratus lumborum

BACK AND SHOULDERS

BODY-WEIGHT CHIN-UPS

Core exercise • Compound/multi-joint
• Pull • Closed chain • Body-weight
• Intermediate to advanced

➡ In the USA, the President's Council on Physical Fitness and Sports sets the following standards for chin-ups:
Men: average = 8; excellent = 13; Women: average = 1; excellent = 8.

Basic description

Pull body up to the bar, at the line of the upper chest. Lower body with control and repeat.

Tips for good form

· Avoid momentum; use controlled movements.
· Avoid hunching or rounding the shoulders. Keep the chest open and the shoulder blades depressed.
· At the bottom, do not hang on the shoulder joint; keep tension in the joint and the mid-back stabilizers active.
· Inhale on the up phase.

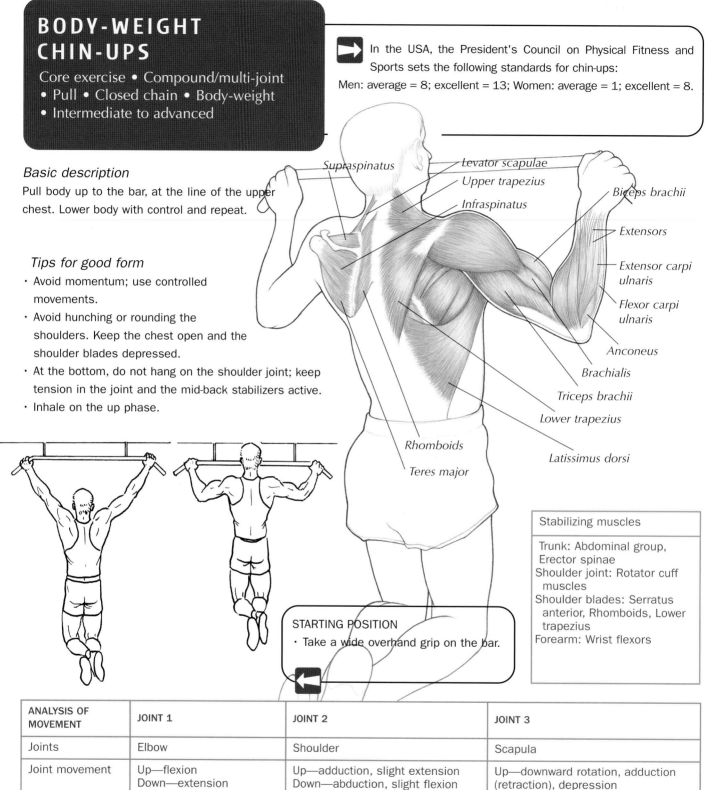

Supraspinatus
Levator scapulae
Upper trapezius
Infraspinatus
Biceps brachii
Extensors
Extensor carpi ulnaris
Flexor carpi ulnaris
Anconeus
Brachialis
Triceps brachii
Lower trapezius
Latissimus dorsi
Rhomboids
Teres major

STARTING POSITION
· Take a wide overhand grip on the bar.

Stabilizing muscles

Trunk: Abdominal group, Erector spinae
Shoulder joint: Rotator cuff muscles
Shoulder blades: Serratus anterior, Rhomboids, Lower trapezius
Forearm: Wrist flexors

ANALYSIS OF MOVEMENT	JOINT 1	JOINT 2	JOINT 3
Joints	Elbow	Shoulder	Scapula
Joint movement	Up—flexion Down—extension	Up—adduction, slight extension Down—abduction, slight flexion	Up—downward rotation, adduction (retraction), depression Down—upward rotation, abduction (protraction), elevation
Mobilizing muscles	Biceps brachii, Brachialis, Brachioradialis	Latissimus dorsi, Teres major, Pectoralis major, Posterior deltoid	Rhomboids, Trapezius

STANDING CABLE PULL-OVER

Auxiliary exercise • Isolated • Pull • Open chain • Machine • Intermediate to advanced

➡️ This exercise, also known as a Straight Arm Pull-down, is particularly useful to strengthen postural stabilizers such as the Abdominals, Serratus anterior, and lower Trapezius. Here, quality of work is more important than quantity.

Basic description

Pull the bar down by extending shoulders until your arms are in line with your sides. Return with control and repeat.

Tips for good form

- Avoid momentum; use a slow, controlled, full range of movement.
- Avoid hunching or rounding the shoulders during the exercise. Keep the chest open and shoulder blades depressed.
- Keep the trunk stable, posture aligned, and spine neutral. You should feel the abdominal stabilizers engaging strongly in the mid-range of movement.
- Exhale on the up phase.

STARTING POSITION

- Stand facing the high cable pulley, one leg in front of the other for better balance, weight 70% on the front leg.
- Take bar with medium grip (slightly wider than shoulder-width).
- Keep posture aligned, spine neutral.

Extensor digitorum

Extensor carpi radialis longus

Brachioradialis

Biceps brachii

Brachialis

Triceps brachii

Deltoid

Infraspinatus

Teres minor

Serratus anterior

Latissimus dorsi

Extensor carpi ulnaris

Anconeus

Teres major

Pectoralis major

Abdominal group

Rectus abdominis

External oblique

ANALYSIS OF MOVEMENT	JOINT 1
Joints	Shoulder
Joint movement	Down—extension Up—flexion
Mobilizing muscles	Latissimus dorsi Teres major Pectoralis major Posterior deltoid

Stabilizing muscles

Trunk: Abdominal group, Erector spinae
Shoulder joint: Rotator Cuff muscles
Shoulder blades: Serratus anterior, Rhomboids, lower Trapezius
Forearm: Wrist flexors

BARBELL BENT-OVER ROWS

Core exercise • Compound/multi-joint
• Pull • Open chain • Barbell
• Intermediate to advanced

➡ Done correctly, this is one of the most valuable and complete upper-body exercises, challenging the postural stabilizing and mobilizing muscles.

Basic description
Pull bar to upper waist. Return and repeat.

Tips for good form
· Avoid momentum; use a slow, controlled, full-range movement.
· Avoid hunching or rounding the shoulders during the exercise. Keep the chest open and shoulder blades depressed.
· Avoid rounding the mid- and lower back. Keep the pelvis neutral, spine aligned.
· Inhale on the up phase.

STARTING POSITION
· Take a stationary squat position over the bar to provide a stable platform.
· Hold bar with a wide overhand grip.

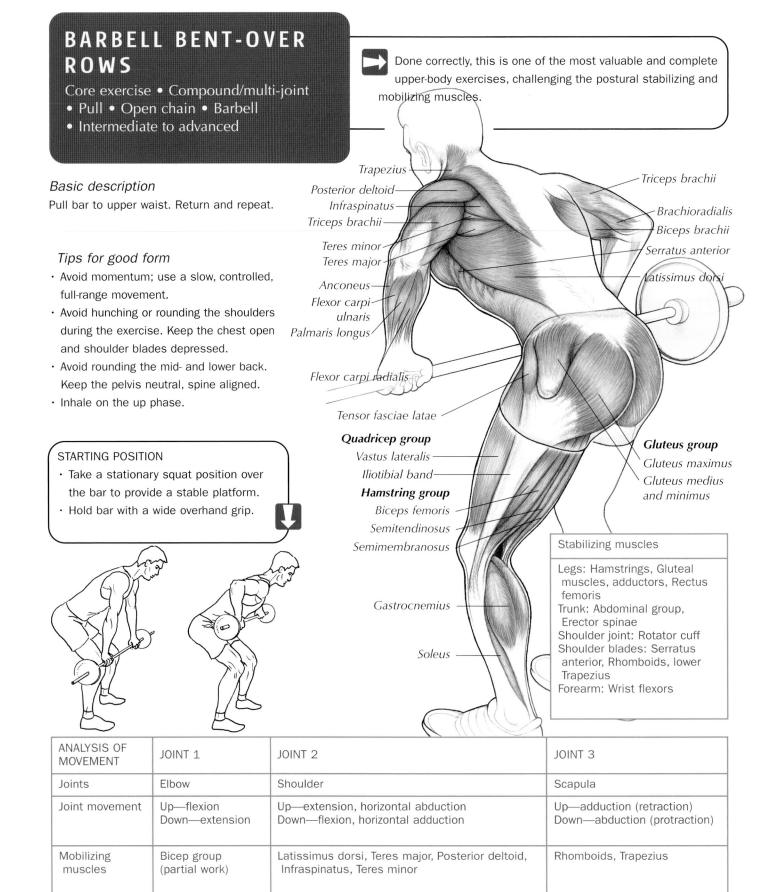

Trapezius
Posterior deltoid
Infraspinatus
Triceps brachii
Teres minor
Teres major
Anconeus
Flexor carpi ulnaris
Palmaris longus
Flexor carpi radialis
Tensor fasciae latae

Triceps brachii
Brachioradialis
Biceps brachii
Serratus anterior
Latissimus dorsi

Quadricep group
Vastus lateralis
Iliotibial band
Hamstring group
Biceps femoris
Semitendinosus
Semimembranosus

Gastrocnemius

Soleus

Gluteus group
Gluteus maximus
Gluteus medius and minimus

Stabilizing muscles

Legs: Hamstrings, Gluteal muscles, adductors, Rectus femoris
Trunk: Abdominal group, Erector spinae
Shoulder joint: Rotator cuff
Shoulder blades: Serratus anterior, Rhomboids, lower Trapezius
Forearm: Wrist flexors

ANALYSIS OF MOVEMENT	JOINT 1	JOINT 2	JOINT 3
Joints	Elbow	Shoulder	Scapula
Joint movement	Up—flexion Down—extension	Up—extension, horizontal abduction Down—flexion, horizontal adduction	Up—adduction (retraction) Down—abduction (protraction)
Mobilizing muscles	Bicep group (partial work)	Latissimus dorsi, Teres major, Posterior deltoid, Infraspinatus, Teres minor	Rhomboids, Trapezius

BENT-OVER ONE ARM DUMB-BELL ROWS

Core exercise • Compound/multi-joint
• Pull • Open chain • Dumb-bell
• Intermediate to advanced

→ This exercise can be likened to the action of sawing wood. Postural stability and a good base position are as important as the mobilizing action.

Basic description

Pull the dumb-bell up to your side until the upper arm is in line with your trunk or just beyond. Return until arm is extended. Repeat. Do alternate sets with opposite arms.

Tips for good form

· Avoid momentum; use a slow, controlled, full-range movement.
· Avoid hunching or rounding the shoulders. Keep the chest open and shoulder blades depressed.
· Avoid rounding or dropping your mid- and lower back. Keep the pelvis neutral and spine aligned.
· Keep your back flat, do not rotate your torso as the arm extends.
· Inhale on the up phase.

Trapezius
Rhomboids
Latissimus dorsi
Infraspinatus
Teres minor
Teres major
Serratus anterior
Abdominal group
External oblique
Rectus abdominis
Posterior deltoid
Triceps brachii
Brachialis
Biceps brachii
Brachioradialis
Pectoralis major
Extensor carpi radialis longus
Anconeus
Extensor carpi radialis brevis

STARTING POSITION

· To be effective, this exercise needs a good, stable base.
· Kneel over a bench with one arm supporting the body, similar to when sawing wood.
· Hold dumb-bell in the opposite hand.

Stabilizing muscles
Triceps: General leg muscles and opposite arm
Trunk: Abdominal group, Erector spinae
Shoulder joint: Rotator cuff muscles
Shoulder blades: Serratus anterior, Rhomboids, lower Trapezius

ANALYSIS OF MOVEMENT	JOINT 1	JOINT 2	JOINT 3
Joints	Elbow	Shoulder	Scapula
Joint movement	Up—flexion Down—extension	Up—extension Down—flexion	Up—adduction (retraction) Down—abduction (protraction)
Mobilizing muscles	Biceps brachii Brachialis Brachioradialis	Latissimus dorsi Teres major Posterior deltoid	Rhomboids, Trapezius

SEATED LOW-CABLE PULLEY ROWS

Core exercise • Compound/multi-joint
• Pull • Open chain • Machine
• Intermediate to advanced

➡️ The first low-cable pulley rowing machines were developed in the late 1940s. This exercise is one of the mainstays of an effective compound back workout.

Basic description
Pull the bar to the waist, keeping the chest open, and shoulders back. Pull so that the arms remain vertical. Return and repeat.

Tips for good form
· Avoid momentum; use a slow, controlled, full range of movement.
· Avoid hunching or rounding the shoulders during the exercise. Keep the chest open and shoulder blades depressed.
· Avoid rounding the mid- and lower back. Keep the pelvis neutral and the spine aligned.
· Inhale on the backward phase.

STARTING POSITION
· Sit on platform; take a close grip on the bar by bending from knees.
· Sit back on the sitting bones, with chest open, and spine aligned.
· Knees remain slightly bent.

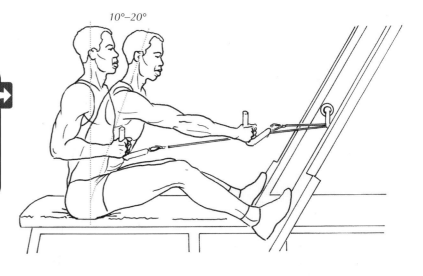

ANALYSIS OF MOVEMENT	JOINT 1	JOINT 2	JOINT 3
Joints	Elbow	Shoulder	Scapula
Joint movement	Back—flexion Forward—extension	Back—extension Forward—flexion	Back—adduction (retraction) Forward—abduction (protraction)
Mobilizing muscles	Biceps brachii Brachialis Brachioradialis	Latissimus dorsi Teres major Posterior deltoid	Rhomboids, Trapezius

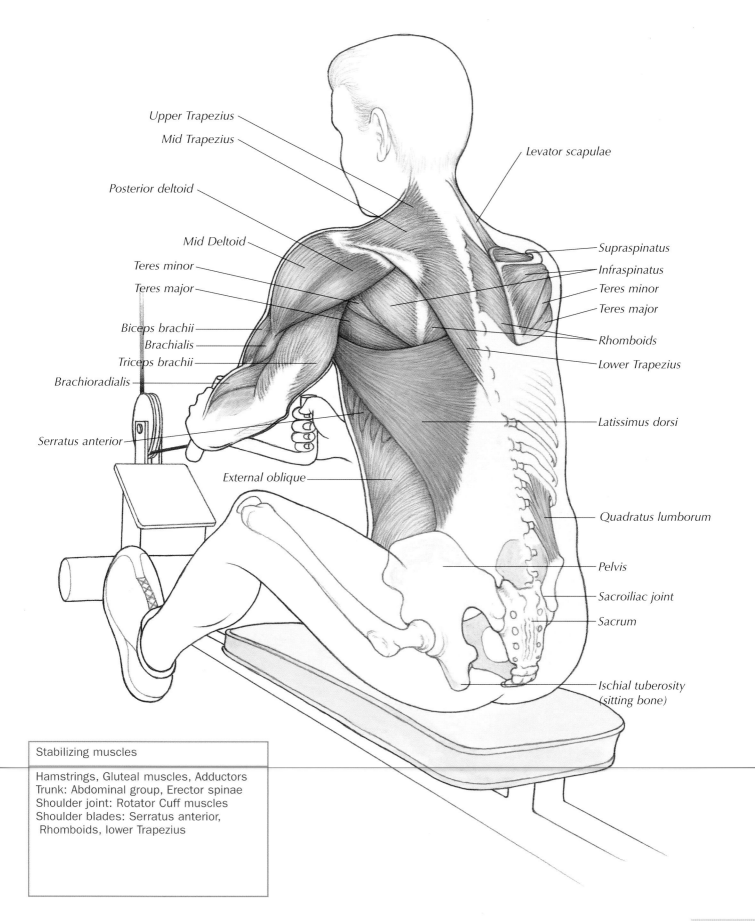

Upper Trapezius

Mid Trapezius

Levator scapulae

Posterior deltoid

Mid Deltoid

Supraspinatus

Teres minor

Infraspinatus

Teres major

Teres minor

Teres major

Biceps brachii

Rhomboids

Brachialis

Lower Trapezius

Triceps brachii

Brachioradialis

Serratus anterior

Latissimus dorsi

External oblique

Quadratus lumborum

Pelvis

Sacroiliac joint

Sacrum

Ischial tuberosity
(sitting bone)

Stabilizing muscles

Hamstrings, Gluteal muscles, Adductors
Trunk: Abdominal group, Erector spinae
Shoulder joint: Rotator Cuff muscles
Shoulder blades: Serratus anterior,
 Rhomboids, lower Trapezius

BACK AND SHOULDERS

PRONE LYING BACK EXTENSION

Auxiliary exercise • Isolated/single joint •
Open chain • Body-weight
• Beginner to advanced

➡ CAUTION: Although this is a seemingly simple exercise, it should not be performed by anyone at risk of lower back injury without professional supervision. Don't cheat by using your glutes instead of your lower back muscles.

Basic description
Use your lower back muscles to slowly lift your shoulders and chest off the floor. Lower and repeat.

Tips for good form
· Avoid momentum; use a slow, controlled, full range of movement.
· Relax the legs and buttocks, and avoid using them to compensate.
· Inhale on the up phase.

Erector spinae

STARTING POSITION
· Lie prone on mat, with arms at your sides.
· Rest your forehead on the floor.
· Relax shoulders, let the chest open.
· Abdominal stabilizers are active.

⬇

ANALYSIS OF MOVEMENT	JOINT 1
Joints	Spine
Joint movement	Up—extension Down—flexion
Mobilizing muscles	Erector spinae

Stabilizing muscles	Trunk: Abdominal group Shoulder blades: Serratus anterior, Rhomboids, lower Trapezius

ANATOMY FOR STRENGTH AND FITNESS TRAINING

BACK EXTENSION APPARATUS

Auxiliary exercise • Compound/multi-joint • Pull • Open chain • Body-weight • Intermediate to advanced

The Back Extension Apparatus provides effective exercise for the back and hip muscles. CAUTION: Do not attempt this without supervision if you suffer from lower back problems.

Basic description

Lower the body to the ground by flexing at the waist, keeping the back straight. Return by raising the body until the trunk is parallel to the legs. Repeat.

Tips for good form

· Avoid momentum; use a slow, controlled, full range of movement.
· Inhale on the up phase.

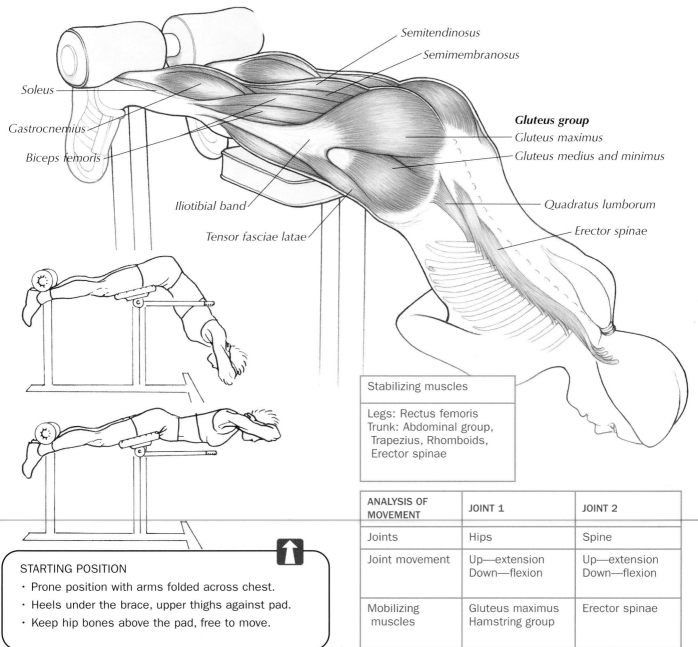

Semitendinosus
Semimembranosus
Soleus
Gastrocnemius
Biceps femoris
Iliotibial band
Tensor fasciae latae

Gluteus group
Gluteus maximus
Gluteus medius and minimus
Quadratus lumborum
Erector spinae

Stabilizing muscles

Legs: Rectus femoris
Trunk: Abdominal group, Trapezius, Rhomboids, Erector spinae

ANALYSIS OF MOVEMENT	JOINT 1	JOINT 2
Joints	Hips	Spine
Joint movement	Up—extension Down—flexion	Up—extension Down—flexion
Mobilizing muscles	Gluteus maximus Hamstring group	Erector spinae

STARTING POSITION

· Prone position with arms folded across chest.
· Heels under the brace, upper thighs against pad.
· Keep hip bones above the pad, free to move.

ALTERNATE ARM/LEG RAISES IN 4-POINT KNEELING

Core exercise • Compound/multi-joint • Push • Closed chain • Body-weight/machine • Intermediate to advanced

As far back as 1983, research showed that 75% of elite athletes complained of back pain at some point in their careers. Among the general public, chronic lower back pain is a leading cause of disability. This exercise can be used in a rehabilitation program for lower back injury, and is an excellent preventative exercise for this condition.

Basic description

Maintaining stabilization and alignment, slowly lift the right leg and left arm simultaneously to the horizontal. Slowly return. Repeat on the opposite side. (Note: the illustration shows the position of the muscles when viewed from above.)

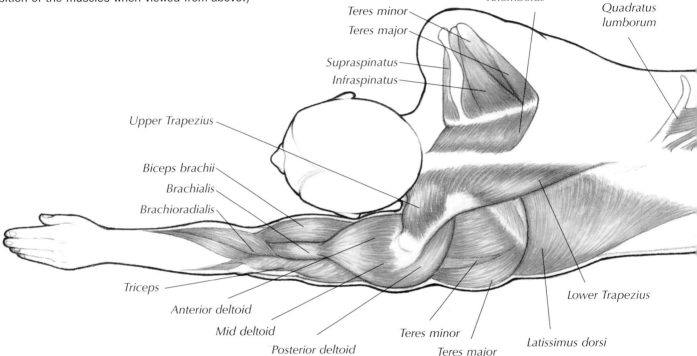

ANALYSIS OF MOVEMENT	JOINT 1	JOINT 2
Joints	Shoulder	Hip
Joint movement	Up—flexion Down—extension	Up—extension Down—flexion
Mobilizing muscles	Posterior deltoid	Gluteus maximus Hamstring group

Stabilizing muscles
Muscles in opposing arm (mainly triceps) and leg Trunk: Abdominal group, Quadratus lumborum, Erector spinae, Adductor group, Gluteus medius and minimus Shoulder joint: Rotator cuff muscles Shoulder blades: Serratus anterior, Rhomboids, lower Trapezius

ANATOMY FOR STRENGTH AND FITNESS TRAINING

Tips for good form

- Avoid momentum; use a slow, controlled, full range of movement.
- Avoid rounding, arching, or twisting the mid- and lower back. Keep the pelvis neutral and the spine aligned.
- Keep the chest open and shoulder blades depressed.
- If you cannot stabilize the trunk, do the exercise while lying prone, or work the arms and legs separately.
- Inhale on the up phase.

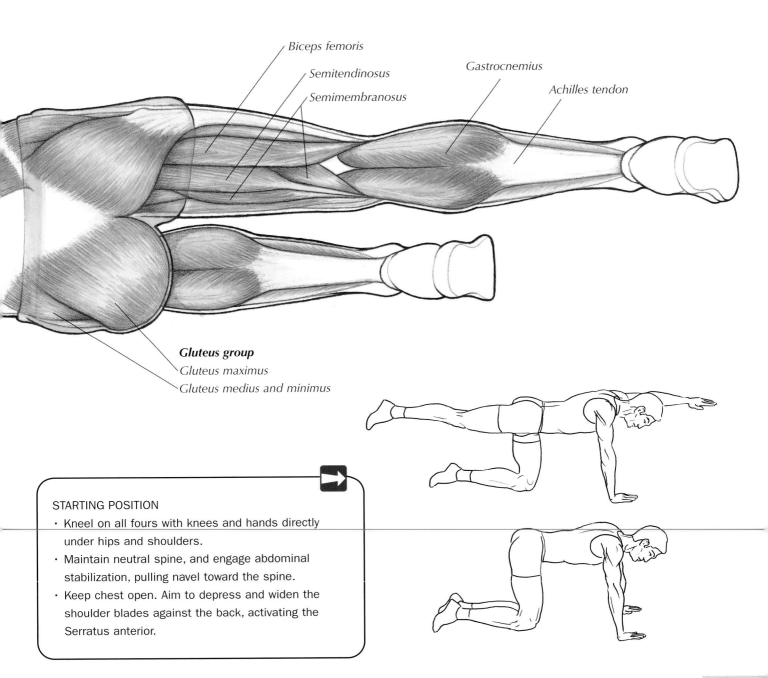

Biceps femoris

Semitendinosus

Semimembranosus

Gastrocnemius

Achilles tendon

Gluteus group
Gluteus maximus
Gluteus medius and minimus

STARTING POSITION
- Kneel on all fours with knees and hands directly under hips and shoulders.
- Maintain neutral spine, and engage abdominal stabilization, pulling navel toward the spine.
- Keep chest open. Aim to depress and widen the shoulder blades against the back, activating the Serratus anterior.

BARBELL SEATED FRONT SHOULDER PRESS

Core exercise • Compound/multi-joint
• Push • Open chain • Barbell
• Intermediate to advanced

➡ This exercise is sometimes referred to as the Overhead or Military Press, the latter name coming from an exercise army troops perform with their rifles during basic training.

Basic description

Raise the bar by extending the arms above the head, then lower it to the upper chest. Repeat.

Tips for good form

· Avoid momentum; use a controlled range of movement.
· Avoid hunching or rounding the shoulders.
· Keep the chest open and shoulder blades depressed.

Pectoralis

Anterior deltoid

Coracobrachialis

Biceps

Latissimus dorsi

Triceps

Brachialis

Abdominal group

External oblique

Rectus abdominis

Serratus anterior

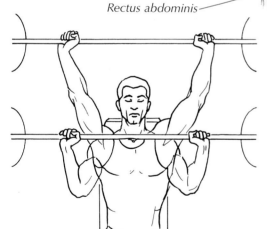

STARTING POSITION

· Sit on the sitting bones, chest open, and spine aligned.
· Hold bar at upper chest height with medium or slightly wider overhand grip.

Stabilizing muscles

Trunk: Abdominal group, Erector spinae
Shoulder joint: Rotator cuff muscles
Shoulder blades: Serratus anterior, Rhomboids, lower Trapezius
Forearm: Wrist flexors

ANALYSIS OF MOVEMENT	JOINT 1	JOINT 2	JOINT 3
Joints	Elbow	Shoulder	Scapula
Joint movement	Up—extension Down—flexion	Up—abduction, flexion Down—adduction, extension	Up—upward rotation Down—downward rotation
Mobilizing muscles	Triceps brachii Anconeus	Deltoid (emphasis on the anterior and mid-fibers) Pectoralis major (clavicular aspect)	Serratus anterior Trapezius

SHOULDER PRESS MACHINE

Core • Compound/multi-joint • Push • Open chain • Machine • Intermediate to advanced

→ The risk of shoulder injury increases when the arm moves from horizontal to abducted and extended. For this reason, overhead press exercises should be introduced gradually. The Shoulder Press Machine is a good option for beginners.

Basic description

Raise machine lever by extending arms. Lower and repeat.

Tips for good form

- Avoid momentum; use slow, controlled movements.
- Avoid hunching or rounding the shoulders.
- Keep the chest open and shoulder blades depressed.
- Exhale on the up phase.

STARTING POSITION
- Sit in machine, holding handles with overhand grip.
- Sit on the sitting bones, chest open, and spine aligned.

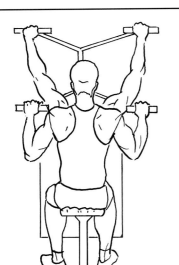

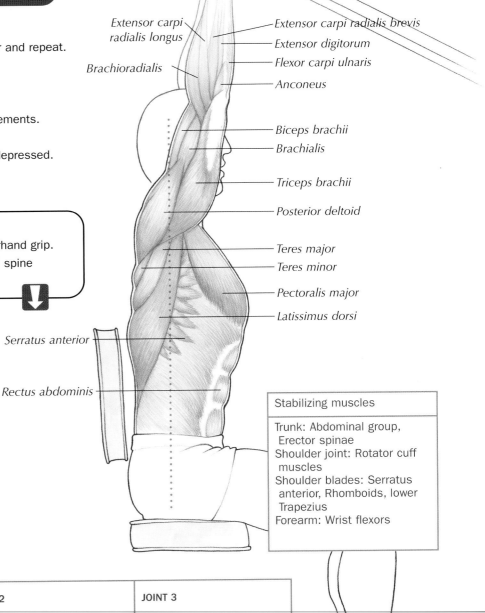

Extensor carpi radialis longus
Brachioradialis
Extensor carpi radialis brevis
Extensor digitorum
Flexor carpi ulnaris
Anconeus
Biceps brachii
Brachialis
Triceps brachii
Posterior deltoid
Teres major
Teres minor
Pectoralis major
Latissimus dorsi
Serratus anterior
Rectus abdominis

Stabilizing muscles

Trunk: Abdominal group, Erector spinae
Shoulder joint: Rotator cuff muscles
Shoulder blades: Serratus anterior, Rhomboids, lower Trapezius
Forearm: Wrist flexors

ANALYSIS OF MOVEMENT	JOINT 1	JOINT 2	JOINT 3
Joints	Elbow	Shoulder	Scapula
Joint movement	Up—extension Down—flexion	Up—abduction, flexion Down—adduction, extension	Up—upward rotation Down—ßdownward rotation
Mobilizing muscles	Triceps brachii Anconeus	Deltoid; Pectoralis major (clavicular aspect)	Serratus anterior Trapezius

SEATED BARBELL PRESS BEHIND NECK

Core exercise • Compound/multi-joint
• Push • Open chain • Barbell
• Advanced

The Seated Barbell Press Behind Neck requires more flexibility from the chest and shoulders than the Barbell Front Press (see p74), and has a more difficult starting position.

Basic description
Raise the bar by extending the arms, then lower it to the upper shoulders, behind the neck.

Lower Trapezius

Posterior deltoid

Infraspinatus
Teres minor
Teres major

Biceps brachii
Brachialis
Extensor carpi radialis
Brachioradialis
Anconeus

Triceps brachii

Latissimus dorsi

Tips for good form

- Warm up before starting. It is recommended that you use a mirror and training partner to "spot" you.
- Avoid momentum; use a slow, controlled, full range of movement.
- Avoid hunching or rounding the shoulders. Keep the chest open and shoulder blades depressed.
- You should have sufficient flexibility not to flex the head excessively forward and the strength for the lift-off at the start.
- Exhale on the up phase.
- CAUTION: Avoid this exercise if you have a history of shoulder dislocations.

STARTING POSITION
- Sit on the sitting bones, chest open, and spine aligned.
- Hold bar with medium or slightly wider overhand grip.

Stabilizing muscles
Trunk: Abdominal group, Erector spinae
Shoulder joint: Rotator cuff muscles
Shoulder blades: Serratus anterior, Rhomboids, lower Trapezius
Forearm: Wrist flexors

ANALYSIS OF MOVEMENT	JOINT 1	JOINT 2	JOINT 3
Joints	Elbow	Shoulder	Scapula
Joint movement	Up—extension Down—flexion	Up—abduction Down—adduction	Up—upward rotation Down—downward rotations
Mobilizing muscles	Triceps brachii Anconeus	Deltoid	Serratus anterior Trapezius

UPRIGHT ROWS WITH EZ BAR

Core • Compound/multi-joint • Pull • Open chain • Barbell • Intermediate to advanced

➡ This traditional shoulder exercise uses the EZ Bar. However, as there is a potential risk of shoulder impingement, it may be contraindicated for people with anterior shoulder problems.

Basic description
Pull the bar up to upper chest height, leading from the elbows. Lower and repeat.

Tips for good form
· Avoid arching from the lower back or at the neck.
· Use a slow, controlled, full range of movement.
· Avoid hunching or rounding the shoulders. Keep the chest open and shoulder blades depressed and retracted.
· Inhale on the up phase.

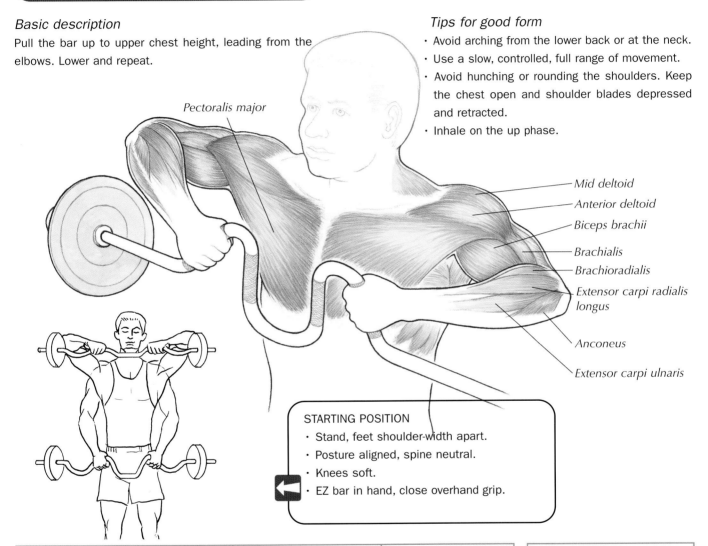

Pectoralis major

Mid deltoid
Anterior deltoid
Biceps brachii
Brachialis
Brachioradialis
Extensor carpi radialis longus
Anconeus
Extensor carpi ulnaris

STARTING POSITION
· Stand, feet shoulder-width apart.
· Posture aligned, spine neutral.
· Knees soft.
· EZ bar in hand, close overhand grip.

ANALYSIS OF MOVEMENT	JOINT 1	JOINT 2	JOINT 3
Joints	Elbow	Shoulder	Scapula
Joint movement	Up—flexion Down—extension	Up—abduction, internal rotation Down—adduction, external rotation	Up—upward rotation Down—downward rotation
Mobilizing muscles	Biceps brachii Brachialis Brachioradialis	Deltoid (emphasis on anterior and lateral aspect)	Trapezius Rhomboids Serratus anterior

Stabilizing muscles
General leg muscles Trunk: Abdominal group and Erector spinae Shoulder joint: Rotator cuff muscles Shoulder blades: Serratus anterior, Rhomboids, and Trapezius Forearm: Wrist extensors

DUMB-BELL STANDING LATERAL RAISE

Auxiliary exercise • Isolated/single joint •
Pull • Open chain • Dumb-bell
• Beginner to advanced

This simple exercise is one of the most biomechanically misunderstood, and is often performed with too much weight and momentum. Done correctly, it is an excellent isolation exercise for the Deltoids.

Basic description

Maintaining a fixed elbow angle of ±10°, raise the arms laterally to shoulder height. Keep the wrist, elbow, and shoulder in line. Lower and repeat.

Tips for good form

· Avoid momentum, especially arching from the lower back. Use slow, controlled, full range of movement.
· Avoid rounding chest and shoulders; keep them open. Depress and widen the shoulder blades against the back, activating the Serratus anterior.
· Doing the exercise with heavier weights and bent elbows is deceiving. By bending the elbow you shorten the effective lever, compensating for additional weight being lifted.
· Inhale on the up phase.

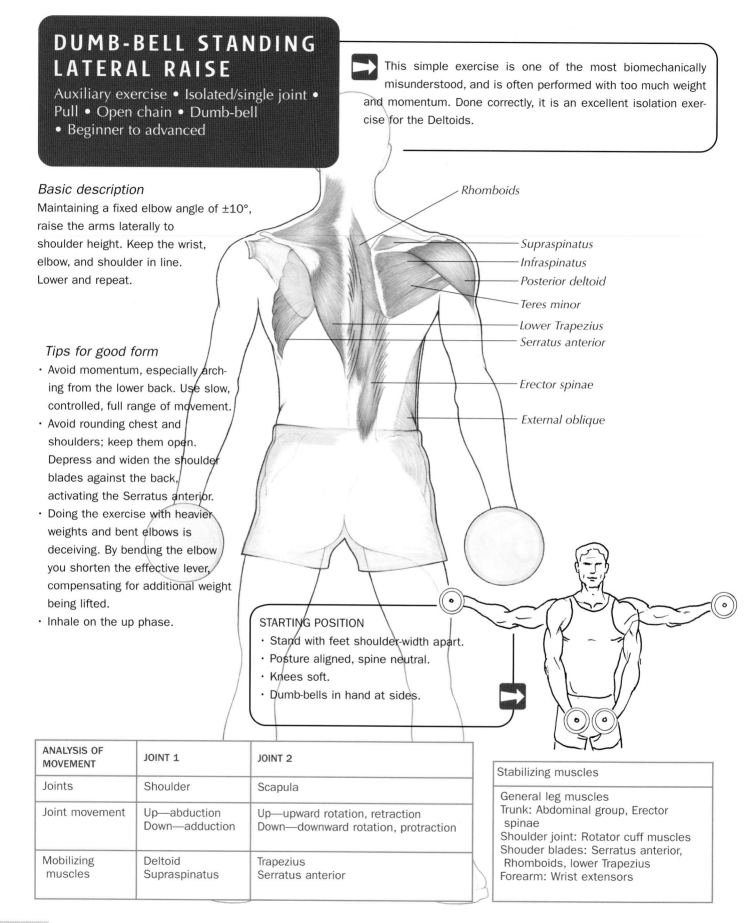

Rhomboids

Supraspinatus
Infraspinatus
Posterior deltoid
Teres minor
Lower Trapezius
Serratus anterior

Erector spinae

External oblique

STARTING POSITION
· Stand with feet shoulder-width apart.
· Posture aligned, spine neutral.
· Knees soft.
· Dumb-bells in hand at sides.

ANALYSIS OF MOVEMENT	JOINT 1	JOINT 2
Joints	Shoulder	Scapula
Joint movement	Up—abduction Down—adduction	Up—upward rotation, retraction Down—downward rotation, protraction
Mobilizing muscles	Deltoid Supraspinatus	Trapezius Serratus anterior

Stabilizing muscles
General leg muscles Trunk: Abdominal group, Erector spinae Shoulder joint: Rotator cuff muscles Shoulder blades: Serratus anterior, Rhomboids, lower Trapezius Forearm: Wrist extensors

DUMB-BELL STANDING FRONT RAISE

Auxiliary exercise • Isolated/single joint •
Push • Open chain • Dumb-bell
• Beginner to advanced

➡ This Dumb-bell Standing Front Raise variation places the emphasis on the Anterior deltoid.

Tips for good form

· Avoid momentum, especially arching from the lower back. Use slow, controlled movements.
· Avoid rounding the chest and hunching the shoulders. Keep them open. Depress and widen the shoulder blades against the back, activating the Serratus anterior.
· Inhale on the up phase.

Basic description

Maintaining a fixed elbow angle of ±10°, raise the arms forward to shoulder-height, keeping the wrist, elbow, and shoulder in line. Lower and repeat.

Anterior deltoid
Pectoralis major
Latissimus dorsi
Serratus anterior

Abdominal group
External obliques
Rectus abdominis

STARTING POSITION

· Stand with feet shoulder-width apart.
· Keep posture aligned, spine neutral.
· Knees soft.
· Hold dumb-bells in front of thighs.

Stabilizing muscles

General leg muscles
Trunk: Abdominal group, Erector spinae
Shoulder joint: Rotator cuff muscles
Shoulder blades: Serratus anterior, Rhomboids, lower Trapezius
Forearm: Wrist extensors

ANALYSIS OF MOVEMENT	JOINT 1	JOINT 2
Joints	Shoulder	Scapula
Joint movement	Up—flexion Down—extension	Up—retraction Down—protraction
Mobilizing muscles	Deltoid (emphasis on the anterior aspect) Pectoralis major (emphasis on clavicular/upper aspect)	Trapezius Serratus anterior

SEATED BENT-OVER DUMB-BELL RAISES

Auxiliary exercise • Isolated/single joint •
Pull • Open chain • Dumb-bell
• Intermediate to advanced

→ In many strength-training programmes, the Posterior deltoid is often overlooked. This exercise is ideal to include in a training program to fill this gap.

Tips for good form

- Avoid momentum, especially lifting the trunk. Use slow, controlled range of movement.
- Keep the chest and shoulders open. Depress and widen the scapulae against the back, activating the Serratus anterior.
- Doing the exercise with heavier weights and bent elbows is deceiving. By bending the elbow you shorten the effective lever, compensating for additional weight being lifted.
- Inhale on the up phase.

Basic description

Maintaining a fixed elbow angle of ±10°–20°, raise the arms perpendicular to the trunk, to shoulder-height. The elbows will be above the line of wrists. Lower and repeat.

Upper Trapezius
Lower Trapezius
Biceps brachii
Brachialis
Posterior deltoid
Triceps brachii
Teres minor
Teres major
Infraspinatus
Rhomboids
Latissimus dorsi
Serratus anterior

Brachioradialis
Anconeus
Flexor carpi ulnaris
Extensor carpi radialis longus

Stabilizing muscles

General trunk muscles
Shoulder joint: Rotator cuff muscles
Shoulder blades: Serratus anterior, Rhomboids, lower Trapezius
Forearm: Wrist extensors

STARTING POSITION

- Sit on edge of bench.
- Position feet farther forward than knees.
- Bring the trunk forward to rest on the knees, as close to horizontal as possible.
- Hold dumb-bells at sides, under the legs.

ANALYSIS OF MOVEMENT	JOINT 1	JOINT 2
Joints	Shoulder	Scapula
Joint movement	Up—horizontal abduction Down—horizontal adduction	Up—retraction Down—protraction
Mobilizing muscles	Posterior deltoid	Rhomboids Trapezius

REAR DELTOID MACHINE

Auxiliary exercise • Isolated/single joint •
Pull • Open chain • Machine
• Beginner to advanced

➡️ Common postural syndromes generally lead to an imbalance between the Anterior and Posterior deltoids, with the former tending to tightness and the latter to functional weakness. The Rear Deltoid Machine strengthens the Posterior deltoid.

Tips for good form

· Avoid momentum, especially arching from the lower back. Use slow, controlled, full range of movement.
· Avoid hunching or rounding the shoulders during the exercise. Keep the chest open and shoulder blades depressed.
· Inhale when pulling back.

Basic description
Maintaining a fixed elbow angle of ±10°, pull the levers backward until elbows are just behind the line of the trunk. Return and repeat.

Levator scapula
Rhomboids
Posterior deltoid
Brachioradialis
Extensor carpi radialis longus
Triceps brachii
Infraspinatus
Teres major
Anconeus
Extensor carpi radialis brevis
Extensor carpi ulnaris
Flexor carpi ulnaris
Lower Trapezius
External oblique
Erector spinae
Latissimus dorsi

STARTING POSITION
· Sit facing the machine.
· Hold the handles at shoulder-height.
· Sit on the sitting bones, with chest open and spine aligned.

⬇️

Stabilizing muscles

Trunk: Abdominal group, Erector spinae
Shoulder joint: Rotator cuff muscles
Shoulder blades: Serratus anterior,
 Rhomboids, lower Trapezius
Forearm: Wrist extensors

ANALYSIS OF MOVEMENT	JOINT 1	JOINT 2
Joints	Shoulders	Scapula
Joint movement	Back—horizontal abduction Forward—horizontal adduction	Back—retraction Forward—protraction
Mobilizing muscles	Posterior deltoid	Rhomboids Trapezius

DUMB-BELL SHOULDER SHRUGS

Auxiliary exercise • Isolated/single joint •
Pull • Open chain • Dumb-bell
• Intermediate to advanced

➡ This is a traditional body-building exercise for strengthening the upper Trapezius.

Basic description

Lift dumb-bells by elevating the scapula and shoulder girdle. Lower and repeat.

Tips for good form

· Avoid momentum, especially arching from the lower back. Use slow, controlled movement.
· Maintain a neutral spine and avoid arching the neck as you elevate the shoulders.
· Keep the chest open.
· Muscles dynamically oppose each other in pairs, such as the lower and upper Trapezius. If the lower Trapezius is under-developed, exercising the upper Trapezius will exacerbate the difference between the two.
· Inhale on the up phase.

Posterior deltoid
Upper Trapezius
Levator scapula
Rhomboids
Supraspinatus
Infraspinatus
Teres minor
Teres major
Triceps
Lower Trapezius
Erector spinae
Serratus anterior
External oblique

⬅ STARTING POSITION
· Stand, with feet shoulder-width apart and knees soft.
· Keep posture aligned, spine neutral.
· Hold dumb-bells at sides.

Stabilizing muscles

Trunk: Abdominal group, Erector spinae
Shoulder joint: Rotator cuff muscles
Shoulder blades: Serratus anterior, Rhomboids, lower Trapezius
Forearms: Wrist flexors

ANALYSIS OF MOVEMENT	JOINT 1
Joints	Scapula
Joint movement	Up—elevation Down—depression
Mobilizing muscles	Upper Trapezius Levator scapula

ROTATOR CUFF STABILIZATION

Auxiliary exercise • Isolation single joint • Push • Open chain • Dumb-bell
• Beginner to advanced

Rotator cuff weakness and imbalance can limit training performance and lead to injuries. This often results in weakness of the external rotators (Supraspinatus, Infraspinatus, and Teres minor), tightness of the internal rotator (Subscapularis), and poor stabilization in general.

Tips for good form
· Work one arm at a time for better focus.
· Avoid momentum. Use slow, controlled, full range of movement.
· Avoid rounding the chest and hunching the shoulder. Keep it open. Depress and widen the shoulder blades against the back, activating the Serratus anterior.
· Keep the elbow at the side but not jammed into the trunk.
· Use moderate/low weight and focus on technique.

Basic description
Maintaining elbow flexion, externally rotate the shoulder. Return and repeat.

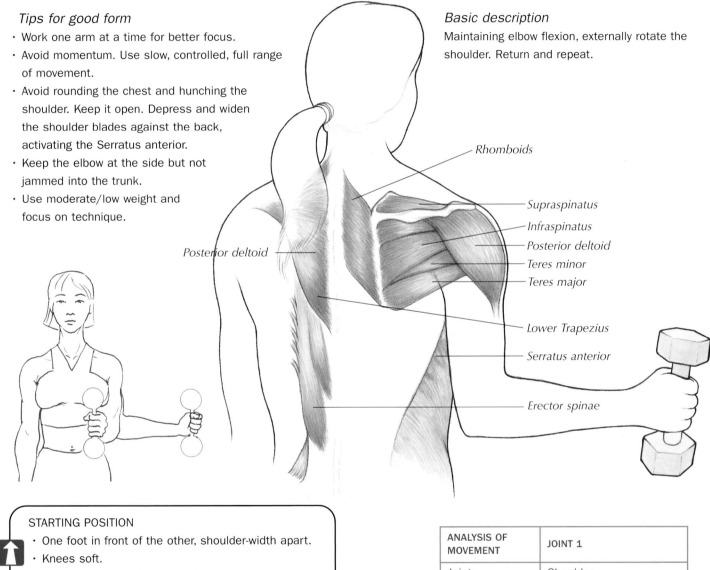

Rhomboids
Supraspinatus
Infraspinatus
Posterior deltoid
Teres minor
Teres major
Posterior deltoid
Lower Trapezius
Serratus anterior
Erector spinae

STARTING POSITION
· One foot in front of the other, shoulder-width apart.
· Knees soft.
· Posture aligned, spine neutral.
· Dumb-bell in hand, elbow flexed at 90°.

ANALYSIS OF MOVEMENT	JOINT 1
Joints	Shoulder
Joint movement	Out—external rotation In—internal rotation
Mobilizing muscles	Infraspinatus Supraspinatus Teres minor Posterior deltoid

Stabilizing muscles	Trunk: Abdominal group, Erector spinae Shoulder blades: Serratus anterior, Rhomboids, lower Trapezius Forearm: Wrist flexors

Major muscles of the forearm

(Note: For purposes of simplicity, some significant muscles are not detailed here. Rotator cuff muscles are listed on p61.)

Name	Joints crossed	Origin	Insertion	Joint
Wrist flexor group				
Flexor carpi radialis	Wrist	Medial epicondyle of the humerus	Anterior surface (palm side) of the second and third metacarpals	Wrist: flexion; abduction (also assists elbow flexion)
Flexor carpi ulnaris	Wrist	Medial epicondyle of the humerus, posterior proximal ulna	Base of the fifth metacarpal, pisiform, and hamate bones	Wrist: flexion; adduction (also assists in weak flexion of the elbow)
Palmaris longus	Wrist	Medial epicondyle of the humerus	Aponeurosis of the palm in the second to fifth metacarpals	Wrist flexion
Wrist extensor group				
Extensor carpi ulnaris	Wrist	Lateral epicondyle of the humerus	Fifth metacarpal dorsal surface (back of the hand)	Wrist: extension; adduction (also assists elbow extension)
Extensor carpi radialis brevis	Wrist	Lateral epicondyle of the humerus	Dorsal surface of the third metacarpal	Wrist: extension; abduction (also assists in elbow extension)
Extensor carpi radialis longus	Wrist	Lateral epicondyle of the humerus	Base of the dorsal surface of the second metacarpal	Wrist: extension; abduction (also assists in weak elbow extension)

Major muscles of the upper arm

Name	Joints crossed	Origin	Insertion	Joint
Bicep group				
Biceps brachii	Shoulder and the elbow	The muscle has two heads: Long head: supraglenoid tubercle, above the glenoid fossa; Short head: coracoid process of the scapula and the upper lip of the glenoid fossa	Tuberosity of the radius	Elbow flexion (best when forearm is supinated); Forearm supination; Assists in shoulder flexion
Brachialis	Elbow	Distal half of the anterior humerus	Coranoid process of the ulna	Elbow flexion
Brachioradialis	Elbow	Distal section of the lateral condyloid ridge of the humerus	Lateral surface of the distal radius, at the styloid process	Elbow flexion; Pronation from supinated position to neutral; Supination from pronated position to neutral

Name	Joints crossed	Origin	Insertion	Joint
Triceps brachii consisting of three divisions with a single insertion: Long head; Lateral head; Medial head	All cross the elbow; the long head also crosses the shoulder	Long head: Lateral side of inferior lip of the glenoid fossa of the scapula; Lateral head: proximal half of posterior humerus; Medial head: Distal two-thirds of posterior humerus	Olecranon process of the ulna	Elbow extension; The long head also performs shoulder extension.
Anconeus	Elbow	Posterior lateral condyle of the humerus	Posterior surface of the olecranon process of the ulna	Elbow extension

Arm muscles

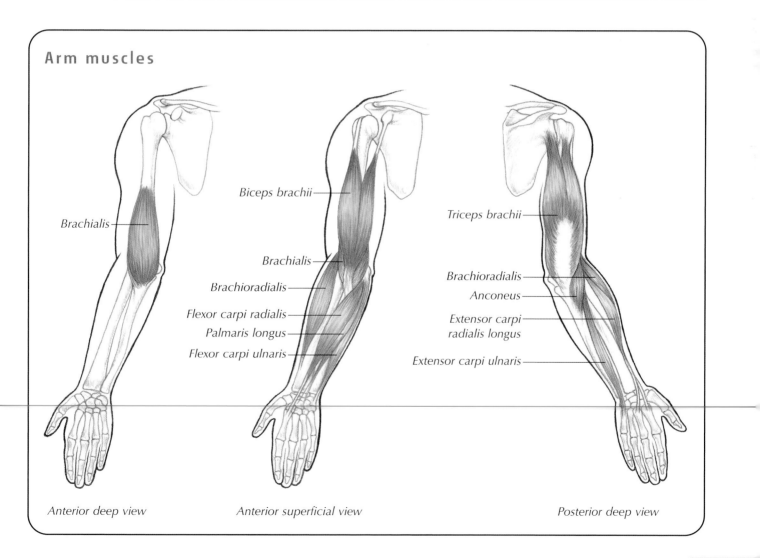

Brachialis

Biceps brachii

Brachialis

Brachioradialis

Flexor carpi radialis

Palmaris longus

Flexor carpi ulnaris

Triceps brachii

Brachioradialis

Anconeus

Extensor carpi radialis longus

Extensor carpi ulnaris

Anterior deep view   *Anterior superficial view*   *Posterior deep view*

DUMB-BELL SEATED OVERHEAD TRICEP EXTENSION ON A BALL

Core • Isolation/ single joint • Push
• Open chain • Dumb-bell
• Intermediate to advanced

This conventional gym exercise is transformed into a more complete and functionally orientated exercise by the use of the stability ball, increasing the role of the stabilizing muscles such as the Abdominals and Erector spinae.

Basic description

Keeping your elbows close to your head, lower the dumb-bell toward the back by flexing the elbow. Return and repeat.

Tips for good form

· Use slow, controlled, motion; avoid momentum.
· This exercise requires significant abdominal stabilization to maintain a neutral spine. Keep the abs engaged, and pull the navel toward the spine.
· Avoid dropping or flaring the elbows outward during movement. The upper arm must be stationary throughout, as though it is part of the spine.
· You can position the wrists closer together to keep the elbows from pointing outward too much.
· Keep the chest open and avoid rounding the shoulders.
· Inhale on the downward phase, exhale up.

STARTING POSITION

· Sit on a stability ball, with posture aligned and stabilized, and with a neutral spine.
· Hold the dumb-bell overhead, arms extended at the shoulder, and grasp the ends of a dumb-bell with your hands.

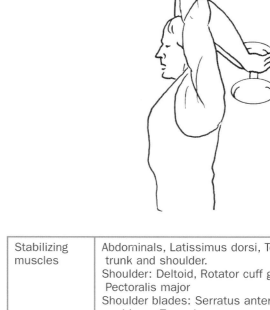

ANALYSIS OF MOVEMENT	JOINT 1
Joints	Elbow
Joint movement	Up—extension Down—flexion
Mobilizing muscles	Triceps brachii (emphasis on the long head) Anconeus

Stabilizing muscles	Abdominals, Latissimus dorsi, Teres major at trunk and shoulder. Shoulder: Deltoid, Rotator cuff group, and Pectoralis major Shoulder blades: Serratus anterior, Rhomboids, and lower Trapeziu. Forearm: Wrist flexors

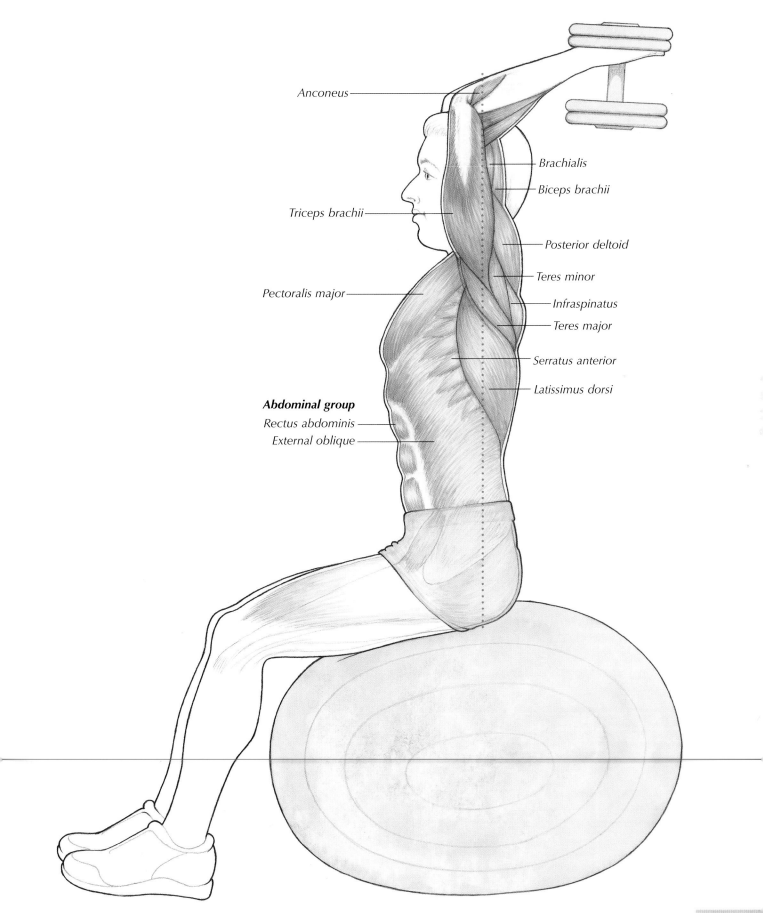

Anconeus

Brachialis

Biceps brachii

Triceps brachii

Posterior deltoid

Teres minor

Pectoralis major

Infraspinatus

Teres major

Serratus anterior

Latissimus dorsi

Abdominal group

Rectus abdominis

External oblique

SUPINE BARBELL FRENCH CURL

Core • Isolated/ single joint • Push • Open chain • Barbell • Intermediate to advanced

➡️ This effective Triceps exercise is often affectionately known as the "headbanger" or "skullcrusher," although these terms are not meant to be taken literally!

Basic description

Lower the bar toward the forehead by flexing the elbows. Stop just before head-level, return, and repeat.

Tips for good form

- Use slow, controlled motion, avoid momentum.
- Avoid dropping or flaring elbows outward. The upper arm must stay stationary throughout the movement.
- Avoid arching the lower back and keep the navel toward the spine.
- Keep the chest open; avoid rounding the shoulders.
- Inhale on the downward phase, exhale on the upward movement.

Biceps brachii
Triceps
Pectoralis major
Coracobrachialis
Posterior deltoid
Teres major
Serratus anterior
Latissimus dorsi

Abdominal group
External oblique
Rectus abdominis

STARTING POSITION

- Lie supine on the bench.
- Arms at shoulder-width or slightly narrower; with overgrip on barbell.
- Barbell in line with forehead, arms extended.

ANALYSIS OF MOVEMENT	JOINT 1
Joints	Elbow
Joint movement	Up—extension Down—flexion
Mobilizing muscles	Triceps brachii (emphasis on the long head), Anconeus

Stabilizing muscles
Abdominals, Latissimus dorsi, Teres major at trunk and shoulder Shoulder: Deltoid, Rotator cuff group, and Pectoralis major Shoulder blades: Serratus anterior, Rhomboids, and lower Trapezius Forearm: Wrist flexors

BARBELL TRICEPS PRESS

Core exercise • Compound/ multi-joint • Push • Open chain • Barbell • Intermediate to advanced

➡️ Essentially, the Barbell Triceps Press is a closed-grip bench press that shifts the emphasis to the Triceps. This is because there is a greater degree of elbow flexion and less shoulder movement than in the Bench Press (see p26).

Tips for good form
- Avoid momentum. Use slow, controlled movements.
- Breathe out when raising the bar.
- Keep chest open, avoid rounding the shoulders.
- Avoid dropping or flaring elbows outward during movement.

Basic description
Bending the elbows, lower the bar to the upper chest, keeping the elbows close to body. Return by pressing until arms are extended. Repeat.

STARTING POSITION
- Lie supine on the bench.
- Take bar from rack with a shoulder-width grip (or slightly narrower).
- Use overgrip on barbell.
- Keep barbell in line with upper chest, arms extended.

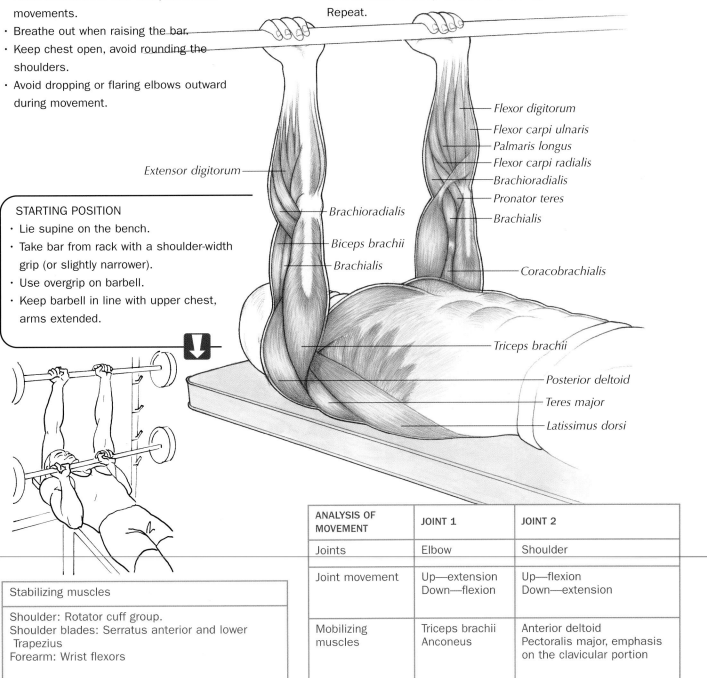

Extensor digitorum
Brachioradialis
Biceps brachii
Brachialis

Flexor digitorum
Flexor carpi ulnaris
Palmaris longus
Flexor carpi radialis
Brachioradialis
Pronator teres
Brachialis
Coracobrachialis
Triceps brachii
Posterior deltoid
Teres major
Latissimus dorsi

Stabilizing muscles

Shoulder: Rotator cuff group.
Shoulder blades: Serratus anterior and lower Trapezius
Forearm: Wrist flexors

ANALYSIS OF MOVEMENT	JOINT 1	JOINT 2
Joints	Elbow	Shoulder
Joint movement	Up—extension Down—flexion	Up—flexion Down—extension
Mobilizing muscles	Triceps brachii Anconeus	Anterior deltoid Pectoralis major, emphasis on the clavicular portion

BENCH DIPS

Core exercise • Compound • Multi-joint •
Push • Close chain • Body-weight •
Intermediate to advanced

➡ An old school favorite wth countless variations. Good stabilization of the scapulothoracic region is particularly important in making this an effective version.

Basic description

Lower your body until your upper arms are parallel to the floor. Return and repeat.

Tips for good form

· Try to keep posture aligned, spine neutral.
· Keep the chest open, avoid rounding and hunching the shoulders. Engage the Serratus and lower Trapezius to do this.
· Inhale on the downward phase, exhale up.
· Slow, controlled motion, avoid momentum.
· Avoid descending too deeply. To protect the shoulder capsule, descend only until the upper arms are parallel to the floor.
· Avoid flaring the elbows outward. Keep the elbows angled posteriorly.

Anterior deltoid

Triceps brachii

Brachialis

Brachioradialis

Anconeus

Pectoralis major

Serratus anterior

Abdominal group

Rectus abdominis

External oblique

Latissimus dorsi

Extensor digitorum

Extensor carpi radialis longus

Extensor carpi radialis brevis

Stabilizing muscles
Shoulder: Deltoid, Rotator cuff group, and Pectoralis major Shoulder blades: Serratus anterior, Rhomboids, and lower Trapezius Forearm: Wrist flexors

ANALYSIS OF MOVEMENT	JOINT 1	JOINT 2
Joints	Elbow	Shoulder
Joint movement	Up—extension Down—flexion	Up—flexion Down—extension
Mobilizing muscles	Triceps brachii Anconeus	Anterior deltoid Pectoralis major

STARTING POSITION
· Place both hands on the edge of a bench, with feet on an adjacent bench, or on the ground (keeping heels flat).

ANATOMY FOR STRENGTH AND FITNESS TRAINING

MACHINE CABLE TRICEP PUSH-DOWN

Auxiliary exercise • Isolated/single joint
• Push • Open chain • Machine
• Beginner to advanced

➡ This is one of the most basic gym exercises for Triceps work as it places emphasis on the medial aspect of the Triceps. To work all portions of the Triceps muscle effectively, you need to use increasingly heavy resistance.

Basic description
Push the bar down by extending at the elbow. Return with control until the forearm is close to the upper arm, and repeat.

Tips for good form
· Use a good range of movement; do not stop the forearm parallel to the ground.
· For better balance with heavy weights, lean forward slightly onto the right leg.
· Avoid flaring elbows outward, keep upper arm stationary, as though it was part of the spine.
· Squeeze from the triceps instead of pushing from the hands.
· Keep chest open, shoulders relaxed, and spine neutral.

➡
STARTING POSITION
· Stand, with legs front and back as opposed to side to side, facing high cable pulley machine.
· Grasp the cable attachment with an overgrip.
· Keep elbows at your sides.
· Shoulders relaxed, spine neutral.

Acromion process
Head of humerus
Scapula
Tricep (long head)
Tricep (short head)
Biceps brachii
Brachialis
Brachioradialis
Extensor carpi radialis longus
Anconeus

ANALYSIS OF MOVEMENT	JOINT 1
Joints	Elbow
Joint movement	Up—extension Down—flexion
Mobilizing muscles	Triceps brachii Anconeus

Stabilizing muscles	Trunk: Abdominals, Erector spinae, Quadratus lumborum Shoulder: Deltoid, Rotator cuff group, and Pectoralis major Shoulder blades: Serratus anterior, Rhomboids, and lower Trapezius Forearm: Wrist flexors

TRICEP ROPE PULL-DOWN

Auxiliary exercise • Isolated/single joint
• Push • Open chain • Machine
• Beginner to advanced

→ This less-common Tricep exercise tends to emphasize the lateral aspect of the Triceps brachii.

Tips for good form

· Use full range of movement, do not stop when the forearm is parallel to the ground.
· Keep posture aligned, spine neutral.
· Inhale on the downward phase, exhale up.
· Chest open, avoid rounding the shoulders.
· Avoid flaring the elbows outward during movement. The upper arm must stay stationary, in line with the spine.
· Use slow, controlled motion and avoid momentum.
· Squeeze from the triceps, instead of pushing from the hands.

STARTING POSITION

· Stand facing the high cable pulley machine.
· Grasp rope attachment with overgrip.
· Keep wrists neutral, thumbs pointing toward each other.
· Keep elbows close to your sides.
· Shoulders relaxed, spine neutral.
· Knees soft.

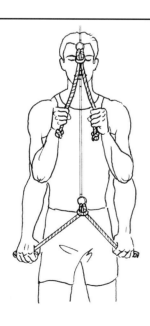

Basic description

Pull the rope down by extending the elbow, using a curvilinear motion, so that the forearms go down to hips first, then curve laterally away, brushing past the side. At the end point, the little finger should point away from body, with the thumbs against the sides. Return with control and repeat.

— Triceps brachii

— Anconeus

Stabilizing muscles

Trunk: Abdominals, Erector spinae, Quadratus lumborum
Shoulder: Deltoid, Rotator cuff group, and Pectoralis major
Shoulder blades: Serratus anterior, Rhomboids, and lower Trapezius
Forearm: Wrist flexors

ANALYSIS OF MOVEMENT	JOINT 1
Joints	Elbow
Joint movement	Extension
Mobilizing muscles	Triceps brachii (emphasis on the lateral aspect) Anconeus

DUMB-BELL KICKBACKS

Auxiliary exercise • Isolated/single joint
• Push • Open chain • Dumb-bell
• Intermediate to advanced

To be effective, this exercise needs a good stable base. Avoid hunching and rounding the shoulders. Use a mirror to help you monitor your form.

Basic description

Extend the arm at the elbow until straight. Return and repeat. Swap sides and repeat.

Tips for good form

· Maintain posture, keep spine neutral.
· Inhale on the downward phase, exhale on the upward phase.
· Keep the chest open, avoid rounding or dropping the shoulders. Also avoid dropping the buttocks.
· Avoid dropping or flaring elbows outward. The upper arm must stay stationary.
· The higher your elbow and the more shoulder extension, the harder the exercise becomes.
· Use slow, controlled motion and avoid momentum.

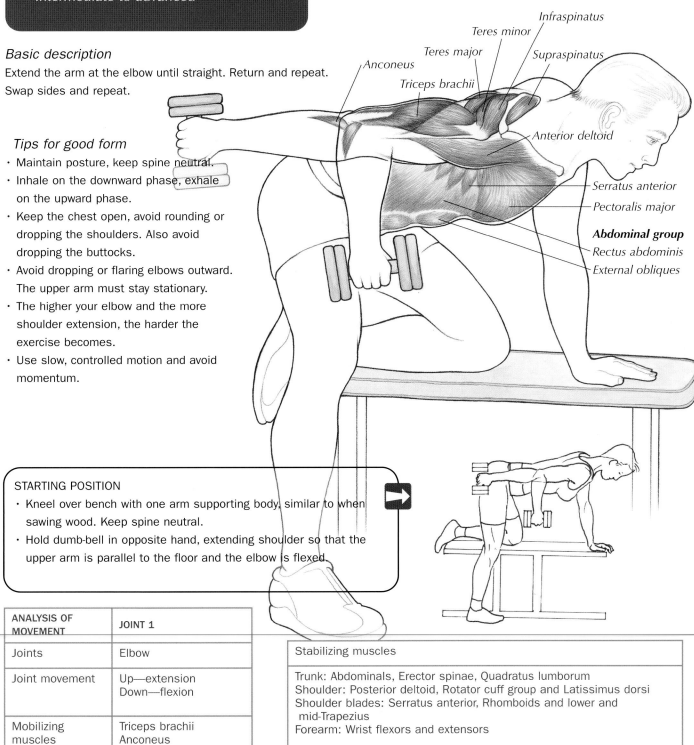

Infraspinatus
Teres minor
Teres major
Supraspinatus
Anconeus
Triceps brachii
Anterior deltoid
Serratus anterior
Pectoralis major
Abdominal group
Rectus abdominis
External obliques

STARTING POSITION

· Kneel over bench with one arm supporting body, similar to when sawing wood. Keep spine neutral.
· Hold dumb-bell in opposite hand, extending shoulder so that the upper arm is parallel to the floor and the elbow is flexed.

ANALYSIS OF MOVEMENT	JOINT 1
Joints	Elbow
Joint movement	Up—extension Down—flexion
Mobilizing muscles	Triceps brachii Anconeus

Stabilizing muscles

Trunk: Abdominals, Erector spinae, Quadratus lumborum
Shoulder: Posterior deltoid, Rotator cuff group and Latissimus dorsi
Shoulder blades: Serratus anterior, Rhomboids and lower and mid-Trapezius
Forearm: Wrist flexors and extensors

STANDING BARBELL CURL

Core exercise • Isolated/single joint
• Pull • Open chain • Barbell
• Beginner to advanced

➡️ This is one of the most effective general bicep exercises. The elbow flexion challenges the Biceps brachii best when the forearms are supinated.

Tips for good form

· Keep posture aligned, spine neutral.
· Use slow, controlled motion, avoid momentum (typically a rocking motion pivoting on the lower back).
· Use full range of movement, do not stop with the forearms parallel with the ground.
· Inhale on the upward phase, exhale down.
· Keep chest open; avoid hunching the shoulders.
· The upper arms must stay stationary throughout, as though they were part of the spine. When elbows are fully flexed, they should only travel forward slightly, so that the forearms are no more than vertical.
· Squeeze from the biceps instead of pulling from the hands, or rocking the lower back.

Basic description

Lift the bar by flexing the elbows until the forearms almost touch the upper arms. Return, lowering the bar until the arms are fully extended. Repeat.

Anterior deltoid
Pectoralis major
Biceps brachii
Serratus anterior
Triceps brachii
Brachialis
Brachioradialis
Extensor carpi radialis longus
Flexor carpi ulnaris
Palmaris longus
Flexor digitorum

STARTING POSITION
· Stand, holding barbell with shoulder-width grip.
· Keep elbows to the side, shoulders relaxed, spine neutral, and knees soft.

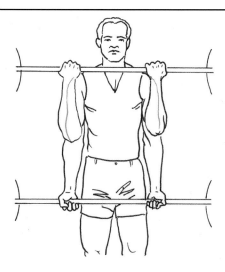

ANALYSIS OF MOVEMENT	JOINT 1
Joints	Elbow
Joint movement	Up—flexion Down—extension
Mobilizing muscles	Biceps brachii Brachialis Brachioradialis

Stabilizing muscles

Trunk: Abdominals, Erector spinae, Quadratus lumborum
Shoulder: Deltoid, Rotator cuff group, and Pectoralis major
Shoulder blades: Serratus anterior, Rhomboids, lower and mid-Trapezius
Forearm: Wrist flexors

ANATOMY FOR STRENGTH AND FITNESS TRAINING

SEATED DUMB-BELL CURL

Core exercise • Isolation/single joint
• Pull • Open chain • Dumb-bell
• Beginner to advanced

➡️ In bicep work, when using a barbell, it is possible to compensate with the stronger arm. Using separate dumb-bells has the advantage of revealing "cheating" by the weaker arm.

Basic description

Lift one dumb-bell by flexing the elbow. At the same time, supinate (turn) the forearm until it is vertical and the palm faces the shoulder. Return and repeat, alternating arms.

Tips for good form

· Keep posture aligned, spine neutral.
· Use slow, controlled motion, avoid momentum.
· Use full range of movement, do not stop with the forearm parallel to the ground.
· Inhale on upward phase, exhale down.
· Keep chest open, avoid rounding or hunching shoulders.
· The upper arms must stay stationary, as though they were part of the spine. When the elbows are fully flexed, they should only travel forward slightly, so the forearms are no more than vertical.
· Squeeze from the biceps, instead of pulling from the hands.

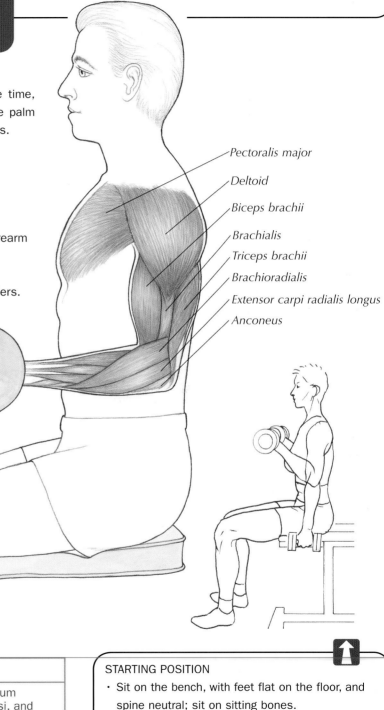

Pectoralis major
Deltoid
Biceps brachii
Brachialis
Triceps brachii
Brachioradialis
Extensor carpi radialis longus
Anconeus

ANALYSIS OF MOVEMENT	JOINT 1
Joints	Elbow
Joint movement	Up—flexion Down—extension
Mobilizing muscles	Biceps brachii Brachialis Brachioradialis

Stabilizing muscles

Trunk: Abdominals, Erector spinae, Quadratus lumborum
Shoulder: Deltoid, Rotator cuff group, Latissimus dorsi, and Pectoralis major
Shoulder blades: Serratus anterior, Rhomboids, lower and mid-Trapezius
Forearm: Wrist flexors

STARTING POSITION
· Sit on the bench, with feet flat on the floor, and spine neutral; sit on sitting bones.
· Hold a dumb-bell in each hand.
· Keep arms to sides, palms facing inward.

BICEP MACHINE CURL

Auxiliary exercise • Isolation/single joint
• Pull • Open chain • Machine
• Beginner to advanced

➡ These machines are not the most effective way of isolating the Biceps, and are often too large for many people. Sitting on a cushion, or raising the seat may help.

Basic description
Lift the weight by flexing the elbow. Return and repeat.

Tips for good form
· Keep posture aligned and spine neutral.
· Use slow, controlled motion, avoid momentum.
· Inhale on the upward phase, exhale down.
· Keep chest open, avoid rounding or hunching the shoulders.
· Squeeze from the biceps instead of pulling from the hands.

STARTING POSITION
· Sit in machine, on sitting bones.
· Hold one machine handle in each hand.
· Keep feet flat and spine neutral. ⬇

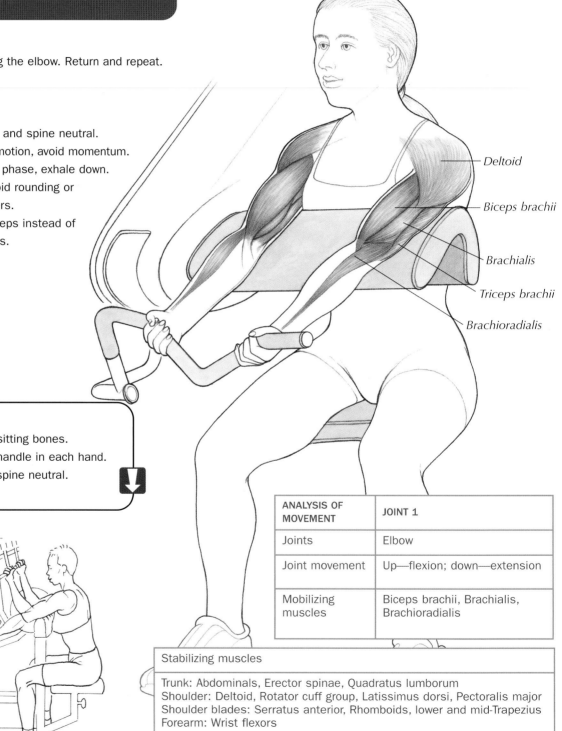

— Deltoid
— Biceps brachii
— Brachialis
— Triceps brachii
— Brachioradialis

ANALYSIS OF MOVEMENT	JOINT 1
Joints	Elbow
Joint movement	Up—flexion; down—extension
Mobilizing muscles	Biceps brachii, Brachialis, Brachioradialis

Stabilizing muscles

Trunk: Abdominals, Erector spinae, Quadratus lumborum
Shoulder: Deltoid, Rotator cuff group, Latissimus dorsi, Pectoralis major
Shoulder blades: Serratus anterior, Rhomboids, lower and mid-Trapezius
Forearm: Wrist flexors

ANATOMY FOR STRENGTH AND FITNESS TRAINING

DUMB-BELL CONCENTRATION CURL

- Auxiliary exercise • Isolated/single-joint
- Pull • Open chain • Dumb-bell •
Intermediate to advanced

 The name of this exercise emphasises both the focus and the intensity of work placed on the Biceps.

Basic description

Lift the dumb-bell toward the front of the shoulder by flexing the elbow. Return, lowering the dumb-bell until arm is fully extended. Repeat. Continue with opposite arm.

Tips for good form

- Keep posture aligned, spine neutral.
- Use slow, controlled motion, avoid momentum.
- Inhale on upward phase, exhale down.
- Keep chest open, avoid rounding or hunching the shoulders.
- Squeeze from the biceps instead of pulling from the hands.

STARTING POSITION
- Sit on bench, legs angled 45° outward, feet flat. Lean forward slightly from the hips.
- Take a single dumb-bell from between feet, placing back of the elbow to inner thigh.
- Have the opposite arm internally rotated, hand palm-down on the thigh to counterbalance frame.
- Maintain neutral spine.

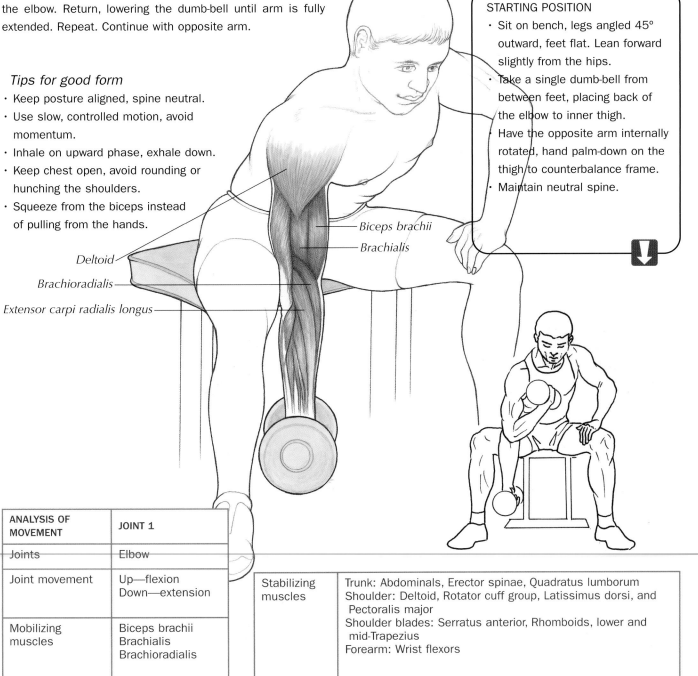

Biceps brachii
Brachialis
Deltoid
Brachioradialis
Extensor carpi radialis longus

ANALYSIS OF MOVEMENT	JOINT 1
Joints	Elbow
Joint movement	Up—flexion Down—extension
Mobilizing muscles	Biceps brachii Brachialis Brachioradialis

Stabilizing muscles	Trunk: Abdominals, Erector spinae, Quadratus lumborum Shoulder: Deltoid, Rotator cuff group, Latissimus dorsi, and Pectoralis major Shoulder blades: Serratus anterior, Rhomboids, lower and mid-Trapezius Forearm: Wrist flexors

BARBELL WRIST CURL

Auxiliary exercise • Isolated/single joint
• Pull • Open chain • Barbell
• Beginner to advanced

When starting gym exercises, many people find their wrists are not strong enough for free-weight training, such as bench presses. This exercise can help strengthen the wrists.

Tips for good form

· Keep posture aligned and spine neutral.
· Use slow, controlled motion; avoid momentum.

Basic description

Let the barbell roll out of the palms down to the fingers. Return by flexing the wrists to return the barbell to the hand. Repeat.

STARTING POSITION

· Sit, leaning forward. Hold the bar with a narrow to shoulder-width underhand grip.
· Rest forearms on thighs, with wrists just beyond the knees.

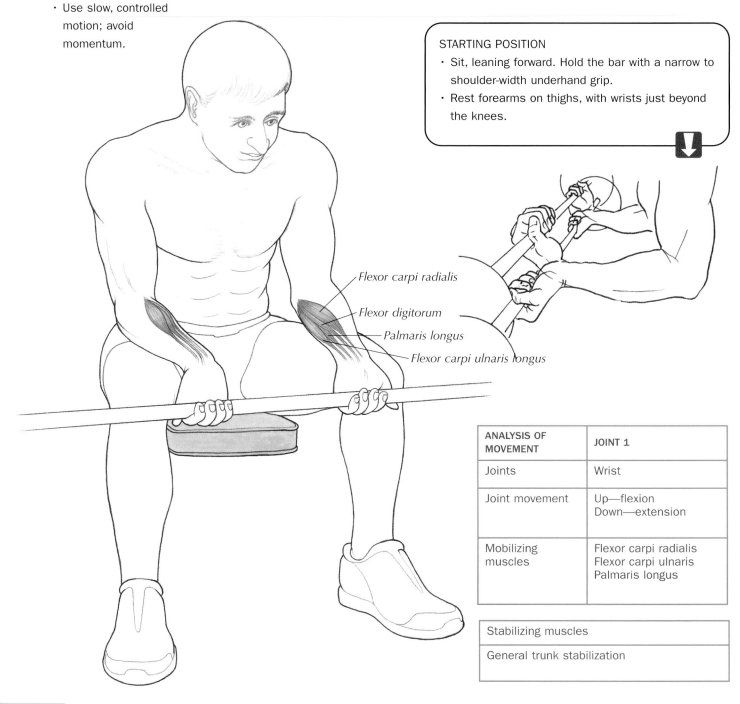

Flexor carpi radialis

Flexor digitorum

Palmaris longus

Flexor carpi ulnaris longus

ANALYSIS OF MOVEMENT	JOINT 1
Joints	Wrist
Joint movement	Up—flexion Down—extension
Mobilizing muscles	Flexor carpi radialis Flexor carpi ulnaris Palmaris longus

Stabilizing muscles
General trunk stabilization

REVERSE BARBELL WRIST CURL

Auxiliary exercise • Isolated/single joint
• Pull • Open chain • Barbell
• Beginner to advanced

➡ This exercise is ideally partnered with Barbell Wrist Curls (see opposite page).

Tips for good form
· Keep posture aligned, spine neutral.
· Use slow, controlled motion; avoid momentum.

Basic description
Extend the wrist, raising the barbell. Return and repeat.

STARTING POSITION
· Sit, leaning forward. Hold the bar with a narrow to shoulder-width overhand grip.
· Rest forearms on thighs, wrists just beyond knees, in flexed position.

⬇

Extensor carpi radialis longus
Extensor carpi radialis brevis
Extensor digitorum

ANALYSIS OF MOVEMENT	JOINT 1
Joints	Wrist
Joint movement	Up—extension Down—flexion
Mobilizing muscles	Extensor carpi radialis longus Extensor carpi radialis brevis Extensor carpi ulnaris

Stabilizing muscles
General trunk stabilization

Major muscles of the lower anterior trunk

Name	Joints crossed	Origin	Insertion	Action
Rectus abdominis	Anterior spine	Crest of the pubis	Xiphoid process and the cartilage of the fifth to seventh ribs	Lumbar flexion (both sides); Lateral flexion to the right (right side); Lateral flexion to left (left side). Controls the posterior tilt of the pelvis (together with External obliques)
External obliques	Anterior spine	Lateral borders of the lower eight ribs	Four aspects: anterior side of the iliac crest; inguinal ligament; crest of the pubis; lower anterior fascia of the rectus abdominis	Lumbar flexion (both sides); Lumbar lateral flexion to the right and rotation to the left (right side); Lumbar lateral flexion to the left and rotation to right (left side); Controls the posterior tilt of the pelvis (together with the Rectus abdominis)
Internal obliques	Anterior spine	Three aspects: upper section of the inguinal ligament; anterior two-thirds of the crest of the ilium; the lumbar fascia	Costal cartilages of the eighth to tenth ribs and linea alba (imagine a V-shape from hips to ribs)	Lumbar flexion (both sides); Lumbar lateral flexion and rotation to the right (right side); Lumbar lateral flexion and rotation to left (left side)
Transverse abdominis	Anterior spine	Four aspects: inguinal ligament; medial rim of iliac crest; medial surface of the lower six rib cartilages; the lumbar fascia	Three aspects: crest of the pubis; iliopectineal line; linea alba. It joins here with the transverse abdominis from the other side	The best type of contraction for this muscle is isometric, drawing the abdomen in toward the spine

Notes:

These muscles are listed in order from most superficial to deepest.

In rotating the trunk, the external and internal Obliques combine (e.g. when the left elbow moves to the right knee, the left external obliques and the right internal Obliques work together to rotate the trunk).

For other stabilizing muscles, see relevant sections.

For many people who exercise, rock-hard abs are a symbol of physical perfection. The abdominals are key stabilizing muscles, helping to maintain neutral posture and alignment, especially of the pelvis and lower back. They help maintain the structural integrity of the digestive and respiratory systems that are held deep to the abdominal wall. For example, laxicity of the abdominals can promote constipation, while shallow breathing patterns promote fatigue.

Other muscles that perform important stabilizing functions are the Gluteal group, Tensor fasciae latae, Rectus femoris, Hamstring group, Iliopsoas, Adductor group, Tibialis posterior in the legs and hips, Erector spinae, lower and mid-Trapezius, Serratus Anterior, Rhomboids, and Rotator cuff group in the back and shoulders. These are muscles whose prime purpose in the body, or in a given movement, is to maintain stability and alignment, so that the effective movement can take place via the mobilizing muscles.

For example, during a Standing Barbell Curl (see p94), the Rotator cuff muscles stabilize and align the shoulder joint, the Abdominal group maintains the alignment of the spine, and the Biceps group perform the isotonic contraction. Certain muscles, by virtue of their position, shape, angle, and structure, are more suited to work as stabilizers than mobilizers.

In functional fitness training (fitness for day-to-day living) we want to train the muscles in the way they were naturally intended to work, that is, to use stabilizers as stabilizers, and mobilizers as mobilizers.

Stabilizers are generally prone to weakness and laxicity. They are best isolated with isometric or small-range movements against heavier resistance or body-weight. They are best worked slowly with long duration. Thus the exercises in this section are more focused toward this kind of training.

Abdominal muscles

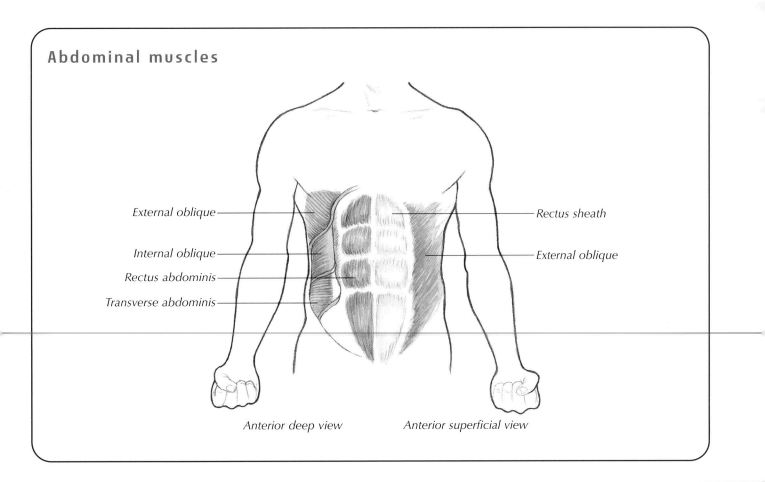

External oblique

Internal oblique

Rectus abdominis

Transverse abdominis

Rectus sheath

External oblique

Anterior deep view

Anterior superficial view

ABDOMINAL STABILIZATION: SITTING AND STANDING

Core exercise • Whole-body stabilization • Beginner to advanced

Stabilizing muscles, such as the abdominals, help to maintain a posture that is balanced against the force of gravity. In this way, the muscles have to do the least work to maintain your posture. We call this a neutral posture.

Try the following basic neutral posture stabilizations:

Standing

- Keep weight balanced through the middle of the feet.
- Keep heels down and imagine lifting your ankles and shin bones.
- Keep knees soft.
- "Pull" your quadriceps up from your knee. As you do so, rotate the upper thigh gently inward. Feel it open space in the lower back.
- Gently lengthen your spine up from your pelvis. Lift and open the chest without sticking the lower border of the ribs forward.
- Pull the shoulder blades down and wide. You'll feel the expansion under your arms.
- Relax arms and shoulders.
- Gently lengthen the neck from the shoulders, balancing the head over the feet. Eyes should look slightly upwards.

Sitting

- Sit on a stability ball and apply the same cues as for standing.
- Activate the abdominal stabilizers by gently squeezing your navel to your spine, without holding your breath.
- Lift one foot off the ground to further challenge your balance and stabilization.

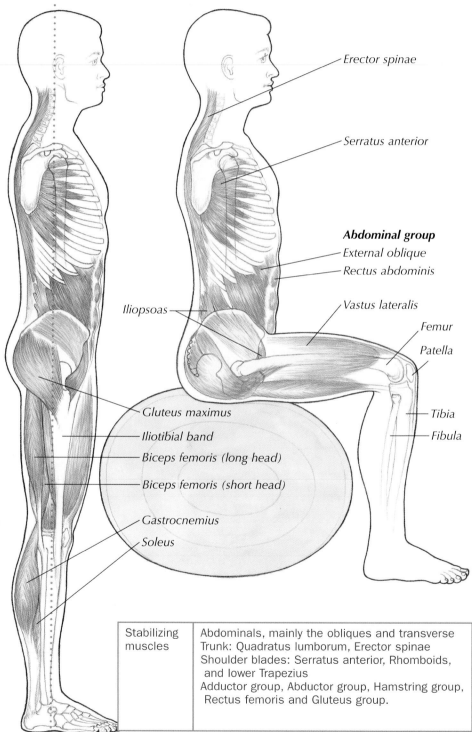

Erector spinae

Serratus anterior

Abdominal group
External oblique
Rectus abdominis

Vastus lateralis

Femur

Patella

Iliopsoas

Tibia

Fibula

Gluteus maximus
Iliotibial band
Biceps femoris (long head)
Biceps femoris (short head)
Gastrocnemius
Soleus

Stabilizing muscles	Abdominals, mainly the obliques and transverse Trunk: Quadratus lumborum, Erector spinae Shoulder blades: Serratus anterior, Rhomboids, and lower Trapezius Adductor group, Abductor group, Hamstring group, Rectus femoris and Gluteus group.

TRANSVERSE ACTIVATION IN 4-POINT KNEELING

Whole-body stabilization • Isolation • Close chain • Body-weight • Focus on abdominals • Beginner to advanced

This exercise helps to create awareness of and strengthen the deepest abdominal, the Transverse abdominus, which helps to keep the abdomen flat and activates expulsion/expiration of the abdominal cavity.

Basic description

Inhale deeply. As you breathe out, squeeze the navel toward the spine, so that you see the abdominals moving upward while the spine itself remains neutral. Relax and repeat.

Tips for good form

· Use a slow, controlled, full range of movement.
· Avoid rounding or arching the mid- and lower back. Keep the pelvis neutral and the spine aligned.
· Keep the chest open and shoulder blades depressed.
· As the transverse moves towards the spine, the waist just above the crest of the hip ("love handles") will seem to get smaller.

STARTING POSITION

· Kneel on all fours, with knees and hands directly under the hips and shoulders.
· Maintain neutral spine.
· Keep chest open. Aim to depress and widen the shoulder blades against the back, activating the Serratus anterior.

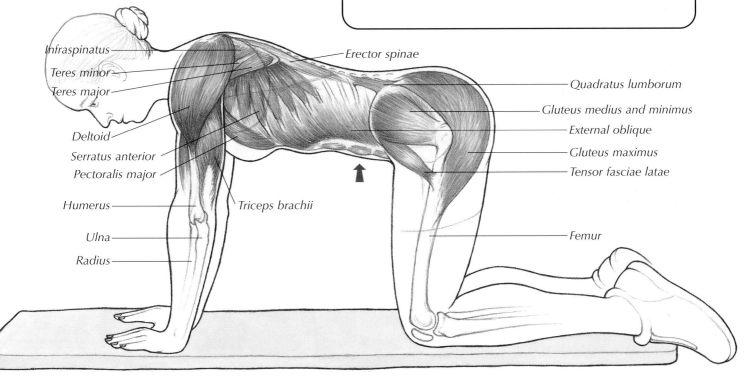

Infraspinatus
Teres minor
Teres major
Deltoid
Serratus anterior
Pectoralis major
Humerus
Ulna
Radius
Triceps brachii

Erector spinae
Quadratus lumborum
Gluteus medius and minimus
External oblique
Gluteus maximus
Tensor fasciae latae
Femur

ANALYSIS OF MOVEMENT	JOINT 1
Joints	Trunk
Joint movement	None
Mobilizing muscles	Transverse abdominal

Stabilizing muscles

Trunk: Abdominals, mainly the Rectus, External and Internal oblique, Quadratus lumborum, Erector spinae, Adductor group, and Gluteus medius and minimus
Shoulder joint: Anterior deltoid, Pectoralis major, Rotator cuff muscles
Shoulder blades: Serratus anterior, Rhomboids, and lower Trapezius
Arm: Triceps

PLANK POSE STABILIZATION

Whole-body stabilization • Focus on abdominals and mid-back stabilizers • Close chain • Body-weight • Intermediate to advanced

 Exercises such as the Plank Pose help to strengthen the stabilizing endurance of the abdominal muscles. This can, in turn, help to reduce the typical lower back pain associated with weak functional stability of the trunk muscles.

Basic description

The primary aim is to maintain stabilization and alignment for a period of time. Start with 10-second intervals and progress to 60 seconds.

Tips for good form

· Avoid rounding or arching the back. Keep the pelvis neutral and the spine aligned.
· Avoid hanging on, or hunching the shoulder blades. Keep the chest open and shoulder blades depressed.
· Do not hold your breath. Breathe in a relaxed manner.

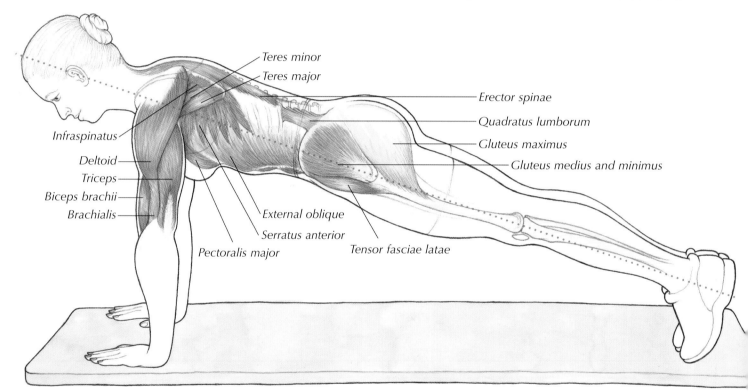

Teres minor
Teres major
Erector spinae
Quadratus lumborum
Gluteus maximus
Gluteus medius and minimus
Infraspinatus
Deltoid
Triceps
Biceps brachii
Brachialis
External oblique
Serratus anterior
Tensor fasciae latae
Pectoralis major

STARTING POSTITION

· Body raised in the prone position, supported on hands and feet (hip-width apart).
· Arms extended, slightly wider than shoulder-width, at the level of the upper chest.
· Maintain neutral spine, engage abdominal stabilization, pulling your navel toward the spine.
· Chest open. Aim to depress and widen the shoulder blades against the back, activating the Serratus anterior and lower Trapezius.

Stabilizing muscles

The Abdominal group
Trunk: Quadratus lumborum, Erector spinae, Adductor group, and Gluteus medius and minimus
Shoulder joint: Anterior deltoid, Pectoralis major, and Rotator cuff muscles
Shoulder blades: Serratus anterior, Rhomboids, and lower Trapezius
Arm: Biceps group and Triceps brachii

FORWARD STABILITY BALL ROLL

Whole-body stabilization • Focus on abdominals, mid-back, shoulder stabilizers • Open chain • Body-weight • Intermediate to advanced

➡️ The stability ball is an inflatable heavy-duty vinyl ball made to withstand repeated use. Introduced in 1909 as a physical therapy tool for children with cerebral palsy, and later used for spinal injuries and back rehabilitation, it entered gym circles in the 1990s.

Basic description

Slowly roll forward maintaining a neutral spine, transverse activation, and shoulder/scapula stabilization. Return and repeat.

Tips for good form

- Avoid momentum. Use slow, controlled, full range of movement.
- The farther forward you go, the longer the lever, and the harder the exercise. Go only to the point where you can maintain effective stabilization, and build up from there.
- Avoid hunching or rounding the shoulders, dropping the hips, or arching the back.
  - Inhale on the forward phase.
  - Start with fewer repetitions and build up.

Supraspinatus
Infraspinatus
Teres minor
Teres major
Biceps brachii
Brachialis
Triceps brachii

Abdominal group
External oblique
Rectus abdominis
Superior anterior iliac crest

Serratus anterior
Latissimus dorsi
Quadratus lumborum
Iliac crest
Pelvis
Coccyx
Ischium
Ischial tuberosity

STARTING POSITION
- Kneeling, legs hip-width apart, in front of the stability ball.
- Place forearms on the ball and lean forward onto it.
- Keep posture aligned and stabilized.
- Shoulders relaxed, chest open, scapula depressed.

ANALYSIS OF MOVEMENT	JOINT 1
Joints	Shoulder
Joint movement	Forward—flexion Return—extension
Mobilizing muscles	Latissimus dorsi Teres major Pectoralis major Posterior deltoid

Stabilizing muscles
The Abdominal group Trunk: Quadratus lumborum, Erector spinae, Adductor group, Gluteus medius and minimus Shoulder joint: Anterior Deltoid, Pectoralis major, and Rotator cuff muscles Shoulder blades: Serratus anterior, Rhomboids, and lower Trapezius Arm: Triceps brachii

BODY-WEIGHT LEANING SIDE ABDOMINAL

Whole-body stabilization • Abdominals, mid- and lower back, shoulder stabilizers • Close chain • Body-weight • Intermediate to advanced

 This exercise brings in the "sideways" stabilizers such as the Gluteus medius and minimus and the Adductors.
CAUTION: It is not recommended for anyone with shoulder or back problems, or with poor stabilization ability.

Basic description

The primary aim is to maintain the stabilization and alignment for a period of time. Start with 5-second intervals and progress to 30-second periods.

Tips for good form

· Keep the shoulders relaxed, scapula depressed, and the abdominals stabilized.
· Avoid letting the top hip rotate forward.
· For an easier version, lower the body to lean on the right elbow.
· Keep the head and neck aligned with the spine.
· Switch over to train both left and right sides.

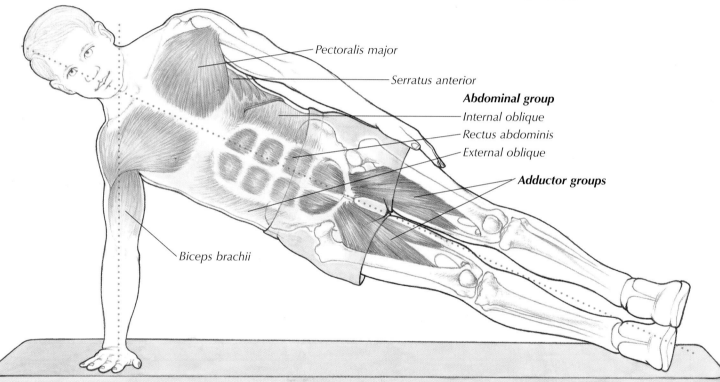

Pectoralis major

Serratus anterior

Abdominal group
Internal oblique
Rectus abdominis
External oblique

Adductor groups

Biceps brachii

Stabilizing muscles

The main stabilizing emphasis is on the Abdominal group, particularly the obliques and transverse abdominus, and the Quadratus lumborum
Trunk: Erector spinae, Adductor group, and Gluteus medius and minimus
Shoulder joint: Deltoid and Rotator cuff muscles
Shoulder blades: Serratus anterior, Rhomboids, and lower Trapezius
Arms: Bicep group and Triceps brachii

STARTING POSITION
· Sit on your right hip, knees bent.
· Keep the shoulder, hip and knee in line.
· Lean on right hand, underneath right shoulder.
· Raise body at the hip, so that the mid-line of the body is straight.

DUMB-BELL SIDE BENDS

Auxiliary exercise • Isolation • Pull
• Open chain • Dumb-bell • Beginner
to advanced

This simple exercise is often misunderstood or incorrectly done. The key to success is to keep slow, controlled mental focus on the mobilizing muscles in order to minimize momentum and to isolate the working muscles.

Basic description

Slowly lower the body to the right by side-bending the trunk. Return slowly and repeat. Change sides and repeat on the left.

Tips for good form

· Avoid momentum. Use slow, controlled movements.
· Avoid hunching or rounding the shoulders. Keep the chest open and the shoulder blades depressed.
· Keep the hips stable over the feet.
· Inhale on the downward movement.
· Focus on isolating the abdominal muscles and lower back muscles on the opposite side of the dumb-bell.
· These muscles are equally active on both up and down movements. Let them out slowly on the way down, and use them to pull the opposite-side ribs on the way up.

Supraspinatus
Rhomboid
Posterior deltoid
Infraspinatus
Teres minor
Teres major
Erector spinae
Triceps brachii
Quadratus lumborum

Gluteus medius and minimus
Femur

ANALYSIS OF MOVEMENT	JOINT 1
Joints	Spine
Joint movement	Down—lateral flexion to the right Up—return
Mobilizing muscles	Rectus abdominis, external Oblique Internal Oblique, Quadratus lumborum (All on side opposite to the dumb-bell)

Stabilizing muscles

The Abdominal group
Trunk: Quadratus lumborum, Erector spinae, Adductor group, and Gluteus medius and minimus
Shoulder joint: Rotator cuff muscles
Shoulder blades: Serratus anterior, Rhomboids, and lower Trapezius

STARTING POSTITION
· Stand with feet shoulder-width apart.
· Keep posture aligned and stabilized.
· Keep knees soft.
· Hold dumb-bell in right hand and place left palm against the head.

BODY-WEIGHT OBLIQUE CRUNCHES

Auxiliary exercise • Isolated • Pull
• Open chain • Body-weight • Beginner to
advanced

 The Oblique Crunch is a simple variation of a crunch that focuses on the External and Internal obliques.

Basic description

Slowly curl the upper body up, bringing the right elbow toward the left knee by flexing and rotating the trunk to the left. The scapula should lift off the mat, while the lower back remains on it, stable and neutral. Pause, return, and repeat. Finish set and change sides.

Tips for good form

- Use slow, controlled, full range of movement and avoid momentum.
- As you lift the body, avoid forcing the chin forward. Keep it tucked in and neutral with the cervical spine as you curl up.
- Avoid pulling the trunk up from the hand or using the shoulder movement to bring the elbow to the knee. Instead activate and isolate the abdominals.
- Don't hunch the shoulders. Keep the chest open and the shoulder blades depressed.
- Exhale on the up phase.

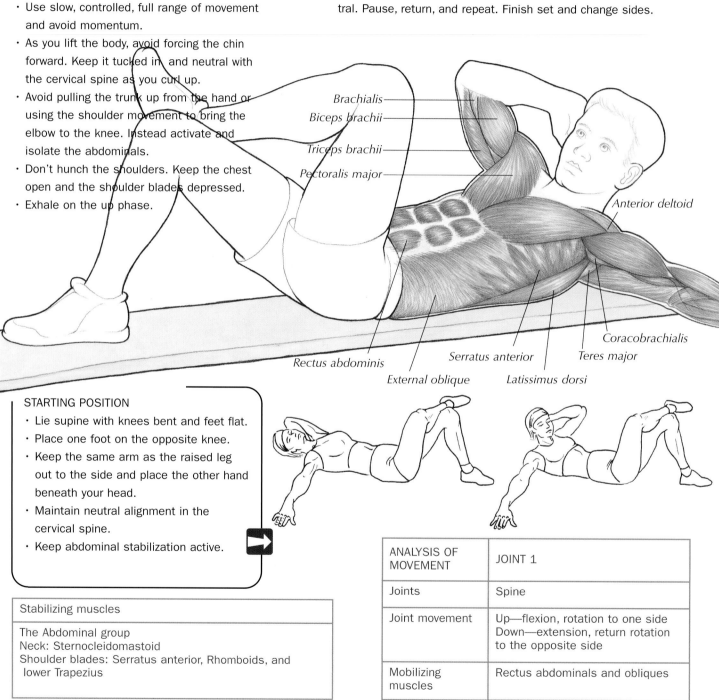

Brachialis
Biceps brachii
Triceps brachii
Pectoralis major
Anterior deltoid
Rectus abdominis
External oblique
Serratus anterior
Latissimus dorsi
Coracobrachialis
Teres major

STARTING POSITION

- Lie supine with knees bent and feet flat.
- Place one foot on the opposite knee.
- Keep the same arm as the raised leg out to the side and place the other hand beneath your head.
- Maintain neutral alignment in the cervical spine.
- Keep abdominal stabilization active.

Stabilizing muscles

The Abdominal group
Neck: Sternocleidomastoid
Shoulder blades: Serratus anterior, Rhomboids, and lower Trapezius

ANALYSIS OF MOVEMENT	JOINT 1
Joints	Spine
Joint movement	Up—flexion, rotation to one side Down—extension, return rotation to the opposite side
Mobilizing muscles	Rectus abdominals and obliques

BODY-WEIGHT CRUNCHES

Auxiliary exercise • Isolated • Pull
• Open chain • Body-weight
• Beginner to advanced

Crunch exercises primarily work the abdominals as a mobilizer. The many variations are useful in any ab training program. (Note: tight back-extensor muscles, such as the Erector spinae, will inhibit peak possible contraction and range of motion in the crunch.)

Tips for good form

- Avoid momentum. Use a slow, controlled full range of movement.
- Avoid forcing the neck or chin to lift the body. Keep the chin tucked in slightly and neutral with the cervical spine as you curl up.
- Avoid pulling the trunk up with the hands. Instead activate and isolate the abdominals.
- Avoid hunching the shoulders. Keep the chest open and the shoulder blades depressed.
- Exhale on the up phase.

Basic description

Slowly curl the upper body upward by flexing the trunk. The scapula should lift off the mat, but the lower back remains on it, stable and neutral. Pause, return, and repeat. (Folding the arms across the chest makes the exercise easier, but will reduce neck support.)

Biceps brachii
Coracobrachialis
Pectoralis major
External oblique
Rectus abdominis
Pubic ramus
Hip socket
Coccyx
Sacrum
Teres minor
Infraspinatus
Teres major
Serratus anterior
Trapezius
Latissimus dorsi

STARTING POSITION

- Lie supine with knees bent and feet flat.
- Clasp hands behind the head.
- Maintain neutral alignment in the cervical spine.
- Keep abdominal stabilization active.

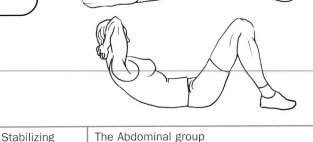

ANALYSIS OF MOVEMENT	JOINT 1
Joints	Spine
Joint movement	Up—flexion Down—extension
Mobilizing muscles	Rectus abdominals and obliques

Stabilizing muscles	The Abdominal group Neck: Sternocleidomastoid Shoulder blades: Serratus anterior, Rhomboids, and lower Trapezius

BODY-WEIGHT SIT-UPS

Core exercise • Compound/multi-joint
• Pull • Open chain • Body-weight
• Intermediate to advanced

Sit-ups have gained a bad reputation, mainly because of poor technique and instruction. Yet, done correctly, this is an effective and advanced compound exercise. The focus should be on quality of movement, not high velocity, or frequent repetitions.

Tips for good form

- Avoid momentum. Use a slow, controlled, full range of movement.
- Avoid forcing the neck or chin forward as you lift the body. Keep the chin tucked in slightly and neutral with the cervical spine as you curl up.
- Avoid pulling the trunk up with the hands. Instead activate and isolate the abdominals.
- Avoid hunching the shoulders. Keep the chest open and shoulder blades depressed.
- Exhale on the up phase.
- Do fewer repetitions without any support, rather than more repetitions with the feet being held. With the feet held and increased velocity, momentum will be generated, leveraged against the lower back. This puts the lower back at risk.

Basic description

Slowly curl the upper body by flexing the trunk. Complete the trunk flexion, bringing the upper body toward the knees. Pause, return slowly, and repeat.

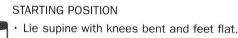

Biceps brachii
Coracobrachialis
Pectoralis major
Rectus abdominis
Coccyx

Teres minor
Infraspinatus
Teres major
Serratus anterior
Trapezius
Latissimus dorsi
Sacrum

STARTING POSITION

- Lie supine with knees bent and feet flat.
- Hands unclasped behind the head.
- Maintain neutral alignment in the cervical spine.
- Abdominal stabilization active.

ANALYSIS OF MOVEMENT	PHASE 1 First ±30° same as crunch range of movement	PHASE 2 Remainder of movement to raise lower back
Joints	Spine	Hip
Joint movement	Up—flexion; Down—extension	Up—flexion; Down—extension
Mobilizing muscles	Rectus abdominals and obliques	Iliopsoas, Rectus femoris
Stabilizing muscles	Neck: Sternocleidomastoid Shoulder blades: Serratus anterior, Rhomboids, and Lower trapezius	Neck: Rectus abdominals and obliques, Sternocleidomastoid Shoulder blades: Serratus anterior, Rhomboids, and lower Trapezius

HIP FLEXOR APPARATUS

Whole-body stabilization • Focus on abdominals, mid- and lower back, shoulder stabilizers • Open chain • Body-weight • Intermediate to advanced

→ People often speak of the Hip Flexor Apparatus as being useful for working the lower abdominals, but this is misleading. While local muscle fatigue is felt in the lower abdominal area, the abdominals work as a whole, contracting isometrically to stabilize and maintain a neutral spine.

Tips for good form

· Avoid momentum. Use slow, controlled movement.
· Don't collapse at the scapula so that the shoulders look hunched. Lift the body up by depressing the scapula through the action of the lower Trapezius and Serratus anterior.
· Keep the chest open in the starting position.
· Inhale on the up phase.
· People with weak abdominal stabilization are unlikely to be able to perform this exercise without acute lower back pain or discomfort.

Basic description

Raise knees to hip height, maintaining stabilized trunk. Return and repeat.

Sternocleidomastoid
Deltoid
Pectoralis major
Biceps brachii
Triceps brachii

Abdominal group
External oblique
Rectus abdominis

Pelvis

Rectus femoris
Iliopsoas

STARTING POSITION
· Support yourself in the apparatus with your weight on your forearms, chest open, spine neutral, and back and buttocks leaning against the backrest.
· Legs dangling, but abdominals stabilizing the pelvis.

ANALYSIS OF MOVEMENT	JOINT 1
Joints	Hip
Joint movement	Up—flexion Down—extension
Mobilizing muscles	Iliopsoas Rectus femoris

Stabilizing muscles	The Abdominal group Neck: Sternocleidomastoid Shoulder blades: Serratus anterior, Rhomboids, and lower Trapezius Shoulder: Rotator cuff group Arm: Biceps brachii, Triceps brachii

ABDOMINALS, STABILIZATION, AND BALANCE

HANGING LEG RAISES

Whole-body stabilization • Focus on abdominals, mid- and lower back, and shoulder stabilizers • Close chain • Body-weight • Advanced

→ This effective but advanced exercise is not suitable for anyone with poor core stabilization ability, or with shoulder or back problems.

Basic description
Raise knees to hip height, maintaining a stabilized trunk. Return and repeat.

Tips for good form
· Avoid momentum. Use controlled movements.
· Avoid collapsing the scapula so that the shoulders look hunched. Raise the body by depressing the scapula through the action of the lower Trapezius and Serratus anterior.
· Keep the chest open.

STARTING POSITION
· Hang from a chin-up bar, with a slightly wider than shoulder grip.
· Keep chest open, spine neutral, and shoulder blades depressed.
· Legs dangle, but abdominals stabilize the pelvis.

←

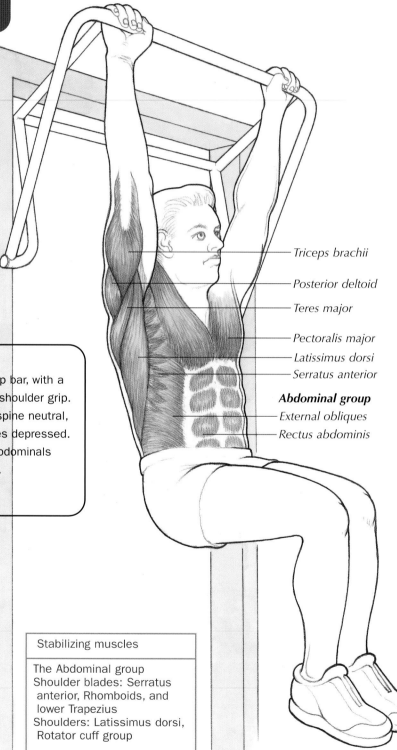

Triceps brachii
Posterior deltoid
Teres major
Pectoralis major
Latissimus dorsi
Serratus anterior
Abdominal group
External obliques
Rectus abdominis

ANALYSIS OF MOVEMENT	JOINT 1
Joints	Hip
Joint movement	Up—flexion; Down—extension
Mobilizing muscles	Iliopsoas Rectus femoris

Stabilizing muscles

The Abdominal group
Shoulder blades: Serratus anterior, Rhomboids, and lower Trapezius
Shoulders: Latissimus dorsi, Rotator cuff group

MID-BACK PRONE SCAPULAR STABILIZATION

Upper-body stabilization • Focus on mid- back stabilizers • Open chain • Body-weight • Intermediate to advanced

→ The scapular stabilizers keep the shoulder blades flat against the back and depressed during upper body exercises. If they are weak, the shoulders hunch, the chest closes and the scapula forms a "wing." This predisposes neck pain and shoulder tension.

Basic description

Lying prone on an incline bench, slowly raise the arms forward and outward with flexed elbows. The palms face toward the head, thumbs pointing to the ceiling. Keep the scapula depressed and shoulders relaxed throughout. Hold for five seconds and return. Repeat.

Tips for good form

· Avoid momentum. Use a slow, controlled movement.
· Avoid hunching the shoulders. Keep the chest open, head and spine neutral, and shoulder blades depressed.
· Elbows should not drop.

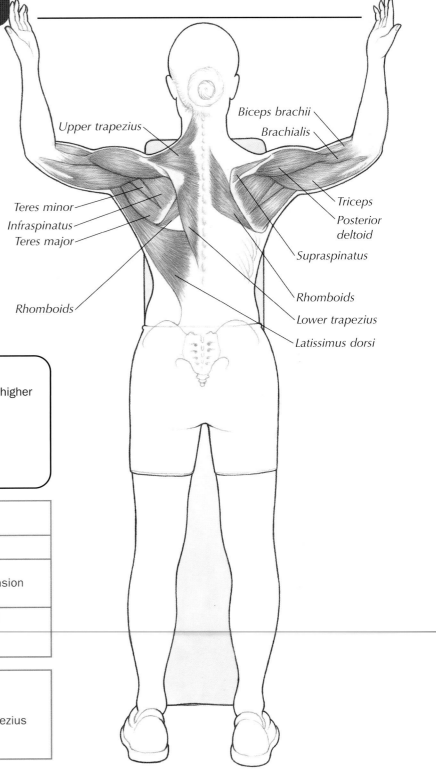

Upper trapezius
Biceps brachii
Brachialis
Teres minor
Infraspinatus
Teres major
Triceps
Posterior deltoid
Supraspinatus
Rhomboids
Lower trapezius
Latissimus dorsi
Rhomboids

STARTING POSITION

· Lie prone against an incline bench, so the head is higher than the feet.
· Stabilize the feet on the ground, keep knees soft.
· Keep posture aligned and stabilized.
· Arms at sides.

ANALYSIS OF MOVEMENT	JOINT 1
Joints	Shoulder
Joint movement	Up—horizontal abduction, flexion Down—horizontal abduction, extension
Mobilizing muscles	Posterior deltoid, Latissimus dorsi Teres major

Stabilizing muscles	The Abdominal group Neck: Sternocleidomastoid Shoulder blades: Serratus anterior, Rhomboids, and lower and mid-Trapezius Shoulder: Rotator cuff group

YOGA TREE POSE

Whole-body stabilization • Body-weight •
Intermediate to advanced

➡ Yoga postures (*asanas*), breathing exercises, and meditation practices reduce stress, lower blood pressure, regulate heart rate, and can even retard the ageing process. These benefits come through increased body awareness, improved posture, flexibility of body and mind, and calmness of spirit.

Begin with the Mountain Pose (Tadasana)

· Start in the basic standing posture (see below left).
· Place the sole of your left foot on the inside of the upper right thigh.
· Open your left knee to the left.
· Keeping the hips square, contract the thigh muscles of the standing leg. Bring your palms together and hold them at the level of your sternum (see below right).
· Once you are balanced, proceed to the Tree Pose.

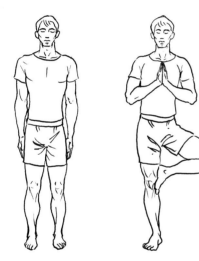

Tree Pose (Vrksasana)

· Proceeding from the Mountain Pose (above right), hold your balance, then raise your arms overhead, with the palms touching (right).
· Press the knee back without moving the hips. Hold for 30 seconds then change sides. Repeat 2–3 sets.

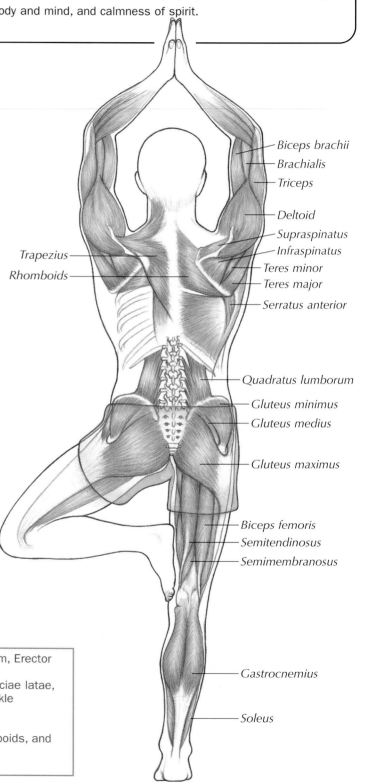

Biceps brachii
Brachialis
Triceps
Deltoid
Supraspinatus
Infraspinatus
Teres minor
Teres major
Serratus anterior
Trapezius
Rhomboids
Quadratus lumborum
Gluteus minimus
Gluteus medius
Gluteus maximus
Biceps femoris
Semitendinosus
Semimembranosus
Gastrocnemius
Soleus

Stabilizing muscles	The Abdominal group: Quadratus lumborum, Erector spinae at the trunk Adductor group, Gluteus group, Tensor fasciae latae, Rectus femoris, Hamstring group, and ankle stabilizers at the lower leg Shoulder joint: Rotator cuff muscles Shoulder blades: Serratus anterior, Rhomboids, and lower Trapezius

ANATOMY FOR STRENGTH AND FITNESS TRAINING

STANDING SQUAT
(BOSU BALANCE TRAINER)

Whole-body stabilization and balance focus • Close chain • Body-weight • Intermediate to advanced

➡️ BOSU is an acronym for "Both-Sides-Up." This balance trainer is like a stability ball cut in half, with a platform on the bottom. It can be used ball-side up to challenge lower-body balance and stability, or platform-side up to target upper-body strength.

Basic description

Standing on the BOSU trainer, flex your knees and squat, as though you are sitting back in a chair. Extend your arms to the front to help maintain your balance. Return to a standing position and repeat.

Tips for good form

· If pelvic stabilization cannot be maintained, lower less than 90° at the knee. Start with as little as 45° flexion.

STARTING POSITION
· Stand on the BOSU with feet slightly forwards of the center.
· Keep knees soft, posture aligned, and stabilized.

Stabilizing muscles

Trunk: Abdominal group, Erector spinae, and Quadratus lumborum
Hips: Gluteus medius and minimus, deep external rotators, and the Adductor group. Ankle stabilizers

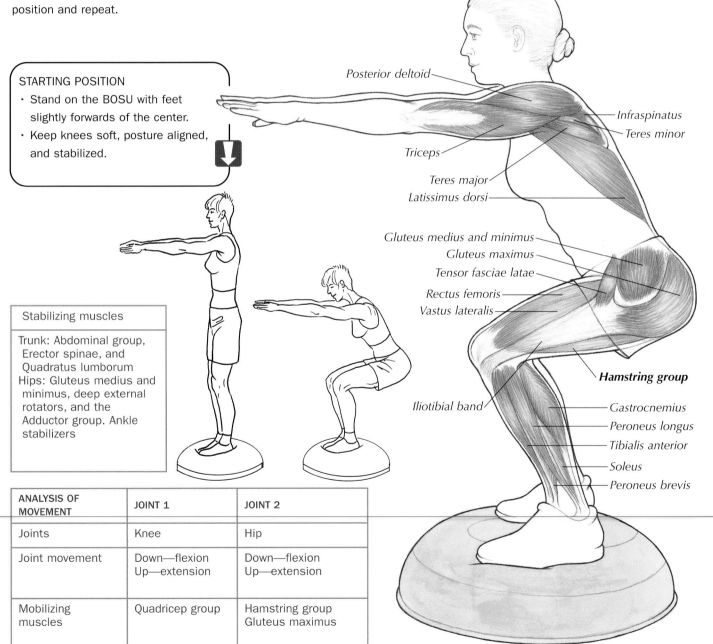

Posterior deltoid
Infraspinatus
Teres minor
Triceps
Teres major
Latissimus dorsi
Gluteus medius and minimus
Gluteus maximus
Tensor fasciae latae
Rectus femoris
Vastus lateralis
Hamstring group
Iliotibial band
Gastrocnemius
Peroneus longus
Tibialis anterior
Soleus
Peroneus brevis

ANALYSIS OF MOVEMENT	JOINT 1	JOINT 2
Joints	Knee	Hip
Joint movement	Down—flexion Up—extension	Down—flexion Up—extension
Mobilizing muscles	Quadricep group	Hamstring group Gluteus maximus

STRETCHING

Stretches and stretching

Flexibility is commonly defined as the range of motion (ROM) around a joint. For each joint there is a degree of flexibility that is considered normal and optimum for daily functioning. Many activities, however, including gymnastics, sprinting, dance, and martial arts, require a greater degree of ROM than is normal for everyday living.

Exercise manuals usually refer to four types of stretching: static, mobilization, Proprioceptive Neuromuscular Facilitation, or PNF, and ballistic (see illustrations opposite).

In static stretches, a progressive mild stretch takes place in a set position. (Most of the stretches analyzed in this section are static stretches.) Mobilization stretching uses a full-range movement around the joint. The PNF technique, which often involves a partner, uses a specific technique to stimulate the muscles and tendons for increased-range work. Ballistic stretching, which incorporates mild bouncing in a static stretch position, is often unfairly maligned, but is useful for elastic strength warm-ups.

Static stretching is relatively safe and is easy to start with. It also makes an ideal cool-down after a workout. Mobilization stretching is the most functional. PNF and ballistic stretching are more advanced, with a higher risk of injury, and are not generally recommended without specialist assessment and instruction.

Benefits of flexibility training

While opinions differ on the benefits of improved flexibility, lack of flexibility is a significant factor in postural compensation, reduced freedom of movement, increased risk of muscle tension, and injury. Some people are naturally more flexible than others, influenced by factors such as gender, genetics, age, and level of physical activity. People who are less active tend to be less flexible and sedentary persons tend to lose flexibility as they age.

The benefits of regular stretching include ease of movement and better postural alignment, the ability to offset age-related loss of flexibility, and a reduced risk of injury and tension.

Conflicting research on stretching may miss the essential relationship between strength and flexibility: muscles work in both agonist and antagonist relationships, that is, some muscles work together and some oppose each other.

In opposing groups, imbalance in one will affect the other. For example, tightness in the Erector spinae will inhibit the abdominal muscles' ability for full-range contraction; and tight Biceps will leave the Triceps in a slightly elongated position.

In cases of significant postural imbalance, some muscles will be tight and some weak. Tight muscles need stretching and weak muscles require strengthening. Many functional training experts agree that one of the best ways to stretch a tight muscle affected by postural imbalance is to strengthen the opposing muscle group. (Remember that adequate assessment is necessary to determine which stretch and strength exercises are necessary for each individual.)

Guidelines for static stretching

- Stretching is best done on warm muscles, as this significantly reduces the risk of injury.
- Ensure proper position and alignment in the starting position.
- Breathe in a relaxed manner; avoid holding your breath, forcing the stretch, or tensing the muscles.
- The stretch should be ±4–7 on a scale of 1–10. At this level, you should feel mild but pleasant discomfort, while 8+ equates to stabbing pain.
- Feel the muscle being stretched, relaxed, and softened. Static stretches should be held for about 30–90 seconds.

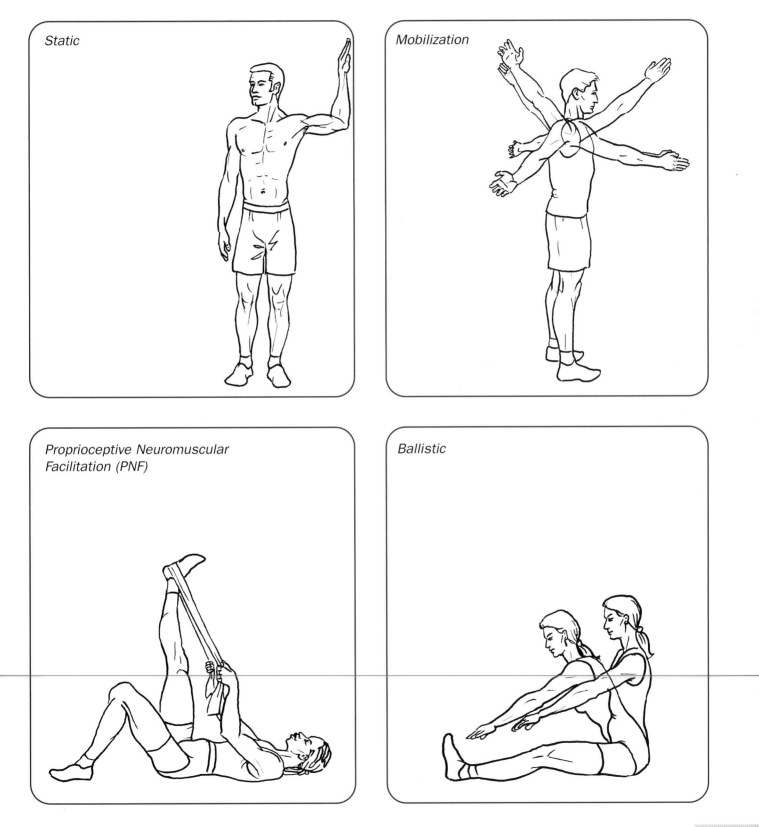

Static

Mobilization

Proprioceptive Neuromuscular
Facilitation (PNF)

Ballistic

STANDING CHEST AND ANTERIOR SHOULDER STRETCH

Static • Isolation/single joint • Close chain • Body-weight • Beginner to advanced

Decreased range of motion (ROM) of the pectorals increases the risk of injury in exercises performed behind the head, such as the Barbell Press Behind Neck (see p76), especially when combined with decreased ROM in the external shoulder rotation.

Basic description

Stand with feet shoulder-width apart and the knees soft, not locked. Keep the posture aligned and stabilized. Extend the arm at shoulder-height, placing the palm onto a doorway. Gently turn the body until you feel a stretch in the chest muscles (±4–7 on a scale of 1–10). Hold the stretch. Repeat with the opposite arm.

Tips for good form

- Avoid forcing the stretch. Relax into it.
- Breathe in a relaxed manner.
- Don't hunch or round the shoulders during the stretch. Keep the chest open, shoulders relaxed, and shoulder blades depressed.
- Avoid locking the elbow; keep elbows extended with a ±10° bend.

Anterior deltoid

Pectoralis major

Abdominal group
External oblique

Rectus abdominis

ANALYSIS OF STRETCH	JOINT 1
Joints	Shoulder
Joint position	Horizontally abducted and externally rotated
Main stretched muscles	Pectoralis major Anterior deltoid External oblique on the side of the arm being stretched

Stabilizing muscles
Abdominal group. Trunk and hips: Quadratus lumborum, Erector spinae, Adductor group, Gluteus medius and minimus Legs: Rectus femoris, Hamstring group, and general leg muscles Shoulder joint: Rotator cuff muscles Shoulder blades: Serratus anterior, Rhomboids, and lower Trapezius

ANATOMY FOR STRENGTH AND FITNESS TRAINING

STANDING TRICEPS STRETCH

Static • Compound/multi-joint
• Close chain • Body-weight • Beginner
to advanced

➡️ While the Triceps brachii is generally not prone to tightness, many of the structures around it are. This stretch incorporates aspects of chest and shoulder flexibility, while also involving the postural stabilizers.

Basic description

Stand with feet shoulder-width apart and the knees soft. Keep the posture aligned and stabilized. Position your right upper arm overhead, and flex the elbow, bringing the right hand to the back of the right shoulder. Place the left hand around the right elbow and gently pull back and toward the head. Hold the stretch at ±4–7 on a scale of 1–10. Repeat with the opposite arm.

Tips for good form

· Avoid forcing the stretch, just relax into it.
· Breathe in a relaxed manner.
· Don't hunch or round the shoulders during the stretch. Keep the chest open, shoulders relaxed, and shoulder blades depressed.
· Avoid collapsing the hips. Activate the abdominal and hip stabilizers, and keep the hips centered over the feet.

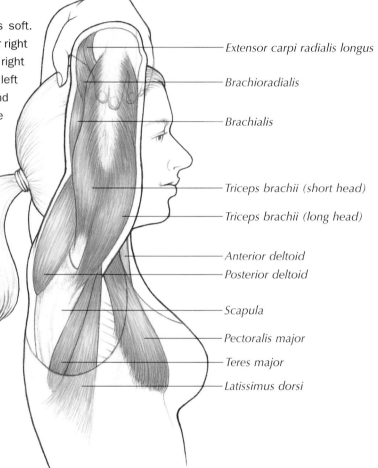

- Extensor carpi radialis longus
- Brachioradialis
- Brachialis
- Triceps brachii (short head)
- Triceps brachii (long head)
- Anterior deltoid
- Posterior deltoid
- Scapula
- Pectoralis major
- Teres major
- Latissimus dorsi

ANALYSIS OF STRETCH	JOINT 1	JOINT 2
Active joints	Shoulder	Scapula
Joint position	Full flexion, i.e. vertical, and externally rotated	Upwardly rotated, and slightly elevated and protracted
Main stretching muscles	Triceps brachii Latissimus dorsi Teres major Posterior deltoid Pectoralis major, emphasis on the abdominal aspect (lower)	Lower Trapezius Lower Rhomboids

Stabilizing muscles

Abdominal group
Trunk and hips: Quadratus lumborum, Erector spinae, Adductor group, Gluteus medius and minimus
Legs: Rectus femoris, Hamstring group, and general leg muscles.
Shoulder joint: Rotator cuff muscles
Shoulder blades: Serratus anterior, Rhomboids, lower Trapezius

SUPINE LEGS TO CHEST

Static • Compound/multi-joint • Body-weight • Beginner to advanced

This basic stretch is ideal to release the typical lower back tension that accumulates from the postural stresses created by daily living. It is also a good warm-up stretch for other supine lower body stretches.

Basic description

Lying supine (on your back, face upward), hug the legs to the chest. Hold at an intensity of ±4–7 on a scale of 1–10. (Note: the main illustration has been manipulated in order to show the muscles used; to do this exercise you must lie on your back, as in the small illustration below.)

Tips for good form

· Avoid forcing the stretch. Relax into it.
· Avoid hunching the shoulders. Keep the chest open, shoulders relaxed, and shoulder blades depressed.
· Breathe in a relaxed manner.

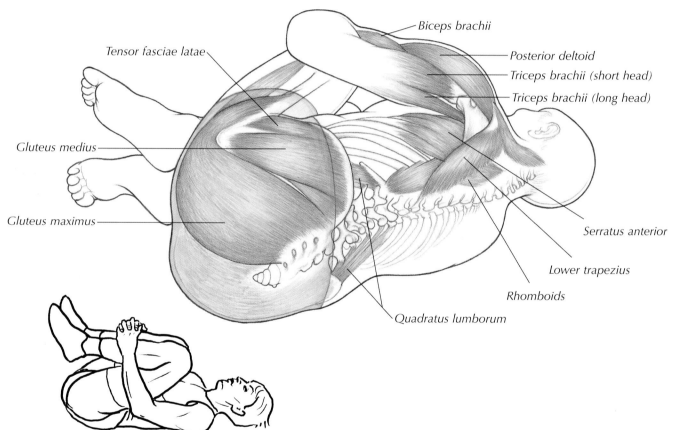

Biceps brachii
Posterior deltoid
Triceps brachii (short head)
Triceps brachii (long head)
Tensor fasciae latae
Gluteus medius
Gluteus maximus
Serratus anterior
Lower trapezius
Rhomboids
Quadratus lumborum

ANALYSIS OF STRETCH	JOINT 1	JOINT 2
Joints	Lumbar spine	Hips
Joint position	Flexed	Flexed
Main stretching muscles	Lower erector Quadratus lumborum	Hamstring group Gluteus maximus

Stabilizing muscles
Arm: Bicep group Abdominal group Shoulder joint: Posterior deltoid, Latissimus dorsi, Teres major, Rotator cuff muscles Shoulder blades: Serratus anterior, Rhomboids, and lower Trapezius

SUPINE GLUTEAL STRETCH

Static • Compound/multi-joint • Body-weight • Intermediate to advanced

➡️ The Gluteus maximus is prone to tightness and weakness, an unusual combination. Tightness increases the risk of lower back strain and injury during typical hip flexion with knee flexion exercises, such as squats and leg presses.

Tips for good form

- Avoid forcing the stretch. Relax into it.
- Breathe in a relaxed manner.
- Avoid hunching or rounding the shoulders during the stretch. Keep the chest open, shoulders relaxed, and shoulder blades depressed.
- If it is not possible to pull the leg to the chest, then leave that step out until your flexibility improves. Instead, keep the right leg crossed over, and push the right knee away slightly with the right hand.

Basic description

Lie supine with both knees bent and feet flat. Cross the right leg over the left, so the right foot is across the left knee. Place both hands around the left thigh and pull it toward the chest until you feel a stretch at ±4–7 out of 10. Hold, then repeat with the other leg.

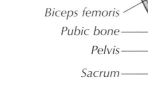

Semimembranosus
Semitendinosus
Vastus lateralis
Biceps femoris
Pubic bone
Pelvis
Sacrum

Iliotibial band
Vastus lateralis
Biceps femoris
Semimembranosus
Triceps brachii
Teres major
Latissimus dorsi
Tensor fasciae latae
Gluteus medius and mimimus
Gluteus maximus

Stabilizing muscles
Arm: Bicep group Shoulder joint: Posterior deltoid, Teres major, Latissimus dorsi, Rotator cuff muscles Shoulder blades: Serratus anterior, Rhomboids, lower Trapezius Abdominal group

ANALYSIS OF STRETCH	JOINT 1	JOINT 2
Active joints	Hip (right thigh)	Hip (left thigh)
Joint position	Flexed, adducted and externally rotated	Flexed
Main stretching muscles	Gluteus maximus Hip: Hamstring group on the lateral aspect	Gluteus maximus Hamstring group

SUPINE SINGLE LEG HAMSTRING STRETCH

Static • Compound/multi-joint
• Open Chain • Body-weight
• Beginner to advanced

→ Hamstring inflexibility increases the risk of lower back strain, especially in exercises where the knees are extended and the hips flexed. If the hamstrings are tight, the lumbar spine will be forced to flex more than normal (this is called postural compensation), placing strain on the joints, and forcing the intervertebral discs toward the posterior.

Basic description

Sit on a mat and place a strap around middle of the right underfoot. Holding the strap evenly in both hands, lie back into the supine position and raise the right leg. Pull the leg vertically, while keeping the knee extended, but not hyper-extended. Keep the opposite leg flexed at the knee, foot flat on the ground. Feel the stretch at ±4–7 on a scale of 1–10. Hold. Repeat with the opposite leg.

Tips for good form

- Avoid forcing the stretch. Relax into it.
- Breathe in a relaxed manner.
- Avoid hunching or rounding the shoulders. Keep the chest open, shoulders relaxed, and shoulder blades depressed.
- To reduce the stretch if hamstrings are very tight, flex the knee of the stretched leg. This also applies if the calf is too tight to allow effective stretching of the hamstring.

Soleus

Gastrocnemius

Hamstring group
Semimembranosus
Semitendinosus

Biceps femoris
Vastus lateralis
Sartorius
Gracilis
Adductor magnus
Iliotibial band
Gluteus maximus

ANALYSIS OF STRETCH	JOINT 1	JOINT 2
Active joint	Hip	Knee
Joint position	Flexed	Extended
Main stretching muscles	Hamstring group Gluteus maximus	Hamstring group Gastrocnemius

Stabilizing muscles
Arm: Biceps group Abdominal group Shoulder joint: Posterior deltoid. Latissimus dorsi, Teres major, Rotator cuff muscles Shoulder blades: Serratus anterior, Rhomboids, and lower Trapezius.

SUPINE DEEP EXTERNAL ROTATOR STRETCH

Static • Isolation • Body-weight
• Intermediate to advanced

➡ Tightness of the deep lateral rotators of the hip is commonly experienced in the dominant leg where it can impinge on the main nerve (sciatic nerve), causing numbness and a tingling sensation down the leg (known as Piriformis syndrome or Sciatica). This stretch has many variants; here, we show the most common form.

Basic description

Lie supine with the legs straight and arms out to the sides. Flex the right knee and hip, and placing the left hand on the lateral (outside) aspect of the right knee, pull the right leg over to the left until you feel a stretch of ±4–7 on a scale of 1–10. The right knee should be in line with, or slightly below, the left hip. Hold. Repeat with the opposite leg.

Tips for good form

· This stretch is advanced, so avoid forcing it. Relax into it.
· If it is not possible to pull over with the arm, let the weight of the leg determine how far it can stretch.
· Make sure the major rotation occurs at the hip before you start to rotate at the lower spine.
· Avoid hunching or rounding the shoulders. Keep the chest open, shoulders relaxed, and shoulder blades depressed.
· Breathe in a relaxed manner.

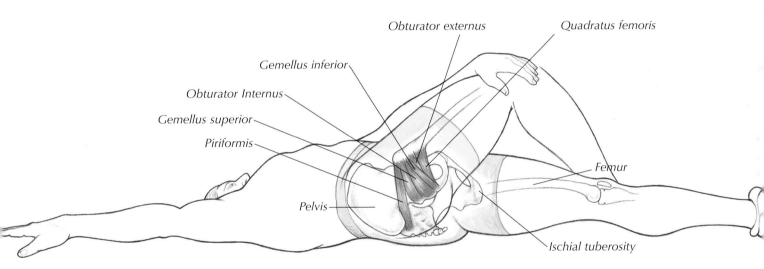

Obturator externus   *Quadratus femoris*
Gemellus inferior
Obturator Internus
Gemellus superior
Piriformis
Femur
Pelvis
Ischial tuberosity

ANALYSIS OF STRETCH	JOINT 1	JOINT 2	Stabilizing muscles
Joints	Hips	Pelvis and spine	Active arm: Tricep group, Posterior deltoid Shoulder joint: Latissimus dorsi, Teres major, Rotator cuff muscles Shoulder blades: Serratus anterior, Rhomboids, lower Trapezius Abdominal group
Joint position	Flexed and horizontally adducted	Rotated	
Main stretching muscles	Deep external hip rotators, namely: · Piriformis · Gemellus superior and inferior · Obturator externus and internus · Quadratus femoris Tensor faciae latae; iliotibial band Gluteus maximus Gluteus medius and minimus	Erector spinae (lower aspect) Abdominal obliques Latissimus dorsi Quadratus lumborum	

SEATED ROTATION

Static • Compound/multi-joint
• Body-weight • Beginner to advanced

 This stretch is an easier option for those who struggle with the more advanced supine hip stretches (see p123).

Tips for good form

· Avoid forcing the stretch. Relax into it.
· Breathe in a relaxed manner.
· Avoid hunching or rounding the shoulders. Keep the chest open, shoulders relaxed, and shoulder blades depressed.
· Sit tall on the sitting bones throughout.
· If your hips are too tight, modify the exercise by sitting on a small cushion or folded towel.

Basic description

Sit tall on the sitting bones, with posture aligned and stabilized. Flex the left knee, keeping the foot on the ground, next to the right knee. Extend the right leg in front, square to the hips. Cross the left foot over the right knee so that the left foot is flat on the ground, lateral to the right knee. Then flex the right knee, so that the right foot tucks up toward the left buttock. Take the right arm around the left knee and hug it toward the chest. Place the left hand on the floor for support. Lengthen and rotate the spine to stretch at an intensity of about 4–7 on a scale of 1–10. Hold. Repeat on the opposite side.

Rectus femoris

Rectus abdominis

Biceps femoris

Femur

Tensor fasciae latae

Gluteus medius

Gluteus maximus

Serratus anterior

External obliques

Stabilizing muscles

The Abdominal group
Trunk: Quadratus lumborum, Erector spinae
Active shoulder joint: Posterior deltoid, Latissimus dorsi, Teres major, Rotator cuff muscles
Shoulder blades: Serratus anterior, Rhomboids, and lower Trapezius

ANALYSIS OF STRETCH	JOINT 1	JOINT 2	JOINT 3
Joints	Hip (of leg being hugged to chest)	Spine	Scapula (on side being hugged to leg)
Joint position	Flexed and inwardly rotated	Rotated towards flexed hip	Protracted
Main stretching muscles	Hamstring group, Gluteus maximus, Deep lateral hip rotators	Abdominal obliques, Quadratus lumborum, Erectors spinae, Latissimus dorsi	Trapezius Rhomboids

KNEELING ILIOPSOAS STRETCH

Static • Isolation • Close chain
• Body-weight • Intermediate
to advanced

➡️ Tightness of the hip flexors, especially the Iliopsoas, can pull the lumbar spine into greater extension during exercises done in a standing position, and this is exacerbated if abdominal stabilization is weak. This exercise is a precise stretch that must be done slowly, with proper attention to technique.

Basic description

Kneel on the right knee, with the left foot forward and the left knee flexed at 90°. The left foot should be flat and underneath, or slightly forward of, the left knee. The hips should be square and the spine aligned and stabilized. Lean the hips gently forward and tilt the pelvis backwards. Place the hands on the hips or on the left knee. Hold, and feel the stretch at an intensity of ±4–7 on a scale of 1–10. Repeat with the opposite leg.

Tips for good form

· Avoid forcing the stretch. Relax into it. You should feel a small tight pull on the front of the hip of the kneeling leg, deep, near to the fold of the leg.
· Breathe in a relaxed manner and keep the posture aligned and stabilized.
· Avoid hunching or rounding the shoulders. Keep the chest open, shoulders relaxed, and shoulder blades depressed.
· Keep the front knee from passing over the vertical line of the toes.

Iliac crest of pelvis

Psoas

Iliacus

Iliopsoas

Rectus femoris

Femur

ANALYSIS OF STRETCH	JOINT 1
Joints	Hip of kneeling leg
Joint position	Extended
Main stretching muscles	Iliopsoas Rectus femoris

Stabilizing muscles	Abdominal group. Trunk and hips: Quadratus lumborum, Erector spinae, Adductor group, Gluteus medius and minimus Legs: Rectus femoris, Hamstring group Shoulder blades: Serratus anterior, Rhomboids, lower Trapezius

SEATED ADDUCTOR STRETCH

Static • Isolation • Body-weight
• Beginner to advanced

 This Seated Adductor Stretch is ideal for beginners, and can later be progressed to obtain a deeper stretch (see below).

Basic description

Sit tall on the sitting bones, with posture aligned and stabilized. Flex the knees and bring the soles of the feet together. You can increase emphasis on the adductors by putting your hands on your feet, positioning the elbows on the medial knee or upper thigh, and adding weight, pressing the upper thighs to floor. Hold at ±4–7 on a scale of 1–10.

Exercise progression

If there is adequate hamstring and calf flexibility, the exercise can be changed to a Stride Sit, where you sit with the legs flat, opened as wide as comfortably possible. Leaning forward from the hips adds a further challenge.

Tips for good form

· Avoid forcing the stretch. Relax into it.
· Avoid hunching or rounding the shoulders. Keep the chest open, shoulders relaxed, and shoulder blades depressed.
· Sit tall. If you lean, lean forward from the hips (as depicted).
· If your hips are very tight, modify the posture by sitting on a small cushion or a folded towel.
· Breathe in a relaxed, calm manner.

Adductor group

Adductor longus

Adductor magnus

Gracilis

Pectineus

Adductor brevis

ANALYSIS OF STRETCH	JOINT 1
Joints	Hips
Joint position	Flexed and externally rotated
Main stretching muscles	Adductor group, namely: · Pectineus · Adductor brevis · Adductor longus · Adductor magnus · Gracilis

Stabilizing muscles	Trunk: Abdominal group and Erector spinae Shoulder blades: Serratus anterior, Rhomboids and lower Trapezius

STANDING GASTROC-NEMIUS STRETCH

Static • Isolation • Close chain
• Body-weight • Beginner to advanced

➡️ The calf muscles have a dense, compact structure, making them suitable for high-volume work. Relative to their size, they are one of the strongest muscles in the body. Frequent stretching is invaluable as tight calves can limit all leg movement.

Basic description

Stand facing a wall, with one foot in front of the other, shoulder-width apart. The front foot is directly underneath a slightly bent knee, while the back leg extends behind. Lean forward and place both arms on the wall at upper chest height. Keeping the feet flat, and posture stabilized, lean the hips into the wall until a stretch of ±4–7 on a scale of 1–10 is felt in the calf muscle. Hold. Repeat with opposite leg.

Tips for good form

· Avoid forcing the stretch. Relax into it.
· Avoid hunching or rounding the shoulders during the stretch. Keep the chest open, shoulders relaxed, and shoulder blades depressed.
· Avoid over-extending the elbow or tensing the shoulders. Keep elbows extended with a ±10° bend.
· Breathe in a relaxed manner.

Semitendinosus
Semimembranosus

Biceps femoris

Gastrocnemius

Soleus

Stabilizing muscles
Trunk: Abdominal group and Erector spinae
Trunk and hips: Adductor group, Gluteus medius and minimus
Shoulder joint: Anterior deltoid, Pectoralis major, Rotator cuff muscles
Shoulder blades: Serratus anterior, Rhomboids, lower Trapezius
Arm: Tricep muscles
Legs: Rectus femoris, Hamstring group, and general leg muscles

ANALYSIS OF MOVEMENT	JOINT 1	JOINT 2
Joints	Ankle (back leg)	Knee (back leg)
Joint movement	Dorsiflexed	Extended
Mobilizing muscles	Gastrocnemius Soleus	Gastrocnemius

TRIANGLE POSE

Static • Compound/multi-joint • Close chain • Body-weight • Beginner to advanced

➡ In Yoga, the Triangle Pose is often practiced as part of a sequence of standing poses used to tone the legs, back, and digestive organs, as well as to develop stability and awareness. It can also be done on its own, as described here.

Basic description

Stand with the feet apart, slightly wider than shoulder-width, and in line, pointing forward. Balancing the weight evenly, rotate the left foot 90°, so that the heel lines up with the arch of the right foot. Stretch the arms out wide to the side, in line with the shoulders and parallel to the ground, palms open. Side flex to the left and slightly upward, rotating the pelvis and trunk. Bring the left fingers down so that the palm touches the foot, ankle, or shin. Stretch the right arm up, bringing it in line with the left arm, and lengthen the spine. Keep the arms, shoulders, hips, and back of the legs aligned in a vertical plane. Hold the pose, then return to the center, and repeat on the opposite side.

Tips for good form

· Avoid forcing the stretch. Relax into it.
· Breathe in a relaxed manner.
· Keep the chest open, shoulders relaxed, and shoulder blades depressed.

Stabilizing muscles	Trunk and hips: Quadratus lumborum, Erector spinae, Adductor group, Gluteus medius and minimus Legs: Hamstring group, Rectus femoris, ankle stabilizers Shoulder blades: Serratus anterior, Rhomboids, lower Trapezius Abdominal group

ANALYSIS OF STRETCH	JOINT 1	JOINT 2	JOINT 3	JOINT 4
Joints	Knees (both legs)	Hip (left side)	Spine	Shoulder (right side)
Joint position	Extended	Abducted, flexed and externally rotated	Lateral flexion	Horizontally abducted and externally rotated
Main stretching muscles	Hamstring group Gastrocnemius	Hamstring group Gluteus maximus	Erector spinae Latissimus dorsi Quadratus lumborum Abdominal group (all on the right side)	Pectoralis major Latissimus dorsi Anterior deltoid

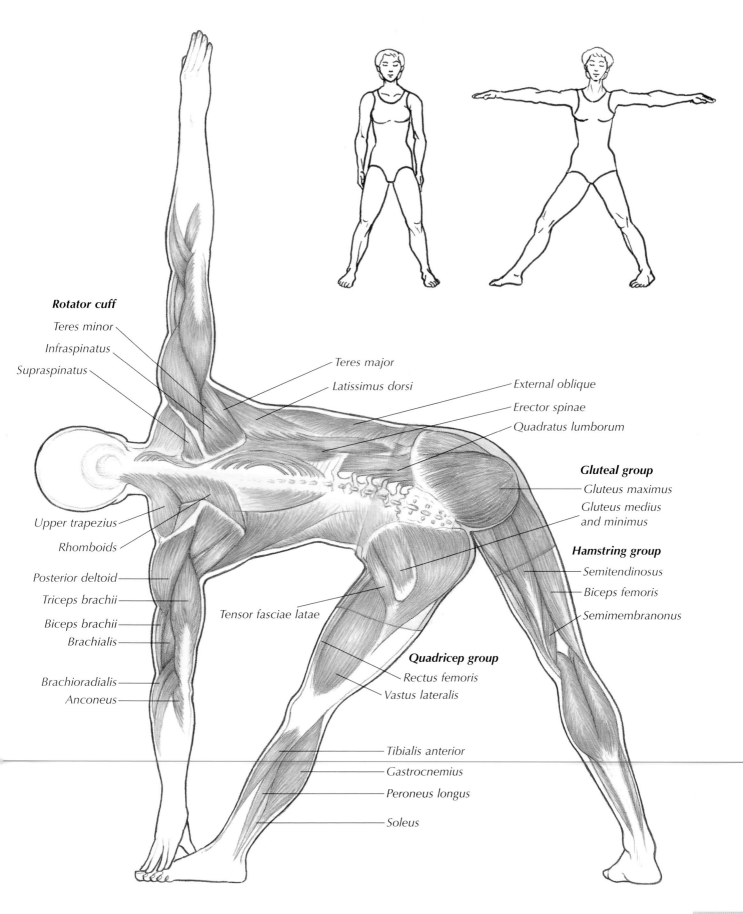

Rotator cuff

Teres minor

Infraspinatus

Supraspinatus

Teres major

Latissimus dorsi

External oblique

Erector spinae

Quadratus lumborum

Gluteal group

Gluteus maximus

Gluteus medius and minimus

Upper trapezius

Rhomboids

Hamstring group

Semitendinosus

Biceps femoris

Semimembranonus

Posterior deltoid

Triceps brachii

Biceps brachii

Brachialis

Tensor fasciae latae

Quadricep group

Rectus femoris

Vastus lateralis

Brachioradialis

Anconeus

Tibialis anterior

Gastrocnemius

Peroneus longus

Soleus

Sample program for developing muscle tone

EXERCISE	SETS	REPS	REST PERIOD	LOAD (on a scale of 1–10)
Barbell Bench Press (pp 26–27)	2–3	12–15	30 sec–2 min	6–7.5
Cable Crossover (p36)	2–3	12–15	30 sec–2 min	6–7.5
Barbell Bent-over Rows (p66)	2–3	12–15	30 sec–2 min	6–7.5
Free-standing Modified Lunge (pp 48–49)	2–3	12–15	30 sec–2 min	6–7.5
Barbell Plié Squat (p45)	2–3	12–15	30 sec–2 min	6–7.5
Machine Seated Leg Extensions (p56)	2–3	12–15	30 sec–2 min	6–7.5
Machine Lying Leg Curl (p57)	2–3	12–15	30 sec–2 min	6–7.5
Barbell Press Behind Neck (p76)	2–3	12–15	30 sec–2 min	6–7.5
Seated Bent-over Dumb-bell Raises (p80)	2–4	12–15	30 sec–2 min	6–7.5
Calf variations	2–4	12–15	30 sec–2 min	6–7.5
Tricep variations	2–4	12–15	30 sec–2 min	6–7.5
Bicep curl variations	2–4	12–15	30 sec–2 min	6–7.5
Abdominal variations	2–4	12–15	30 sec–2 min	6–7.5

Sample program for developing functional strength

EXERCISE	SETS	REPS	REST PERIOD	LOAD (on a scale of 1–10)
Rotator Cuff Stabilization (p83)	2–3	12–30	30 sec–2 min	3–8
Push-ups (pp 28–29)	2–3	12–30	30 sec–2 min	3–8
Body-weight Dips (p35)	2–3	12–30	30 sec–2 min	3–8
Double-leg Bridge (p50)	2–3	12–30	30 sec–2 min	3–8
Barbell Bent-over Rows (p66)	2–3	12–30	30 sec–2 min	3–8
Standing Cable Pullover (p65)	2–3	12–30	30 sec–2 min	3–8
Alternate Arm Leg Raises (pp 72–73)	2	12–30	30 sec–2 min	3–8
Dumb-bell Seated Tricep Extension (pp 86–87)	2–3	12–30	30 sec–2 min	3–8
Transverse Activation (p103)	2	12–30	30 sec–2 min	3–8

ANATOMY FOR STRENGTH AND FITNESS TRAINING

TOTAL BODY AND POWER EXERCISES

This section focuses on the explosive power exercises typified in the sport of power-lifting: the Clean and Jerk, the Snatch, and the Dead Lift. Power is a combination of strength and speed; so a powerful or explosive movement is one that involves relatively fast, forceful actions.

Weights lifted can be measured in terms of percentage of one repetition max (the maximum weight you can lift properly, in a given exercise, once only).

In power training it is generally agreed that lower weights (±30%) and higher velocity improve the speed aspect, while workloads greater than 60% improve the strength component. Between 30% and 60% of maximum will divide any improvements between both components

Power training works on the reactive capacity of the neural systems and the coordination of the motor units. New stressors are applied to the tendons, while ligaments and joint structures will have more instability stress due to the increased momentum.

It takes time to adapt to power exercise, so beginners should work with lower weights (±30% of body weight) and focus on achieving good form. Avoid extremes of velocity or the amount of weight lifted, as these dramatically increase the injury risk. Power exercises should be limited to sets of five repetitions in one training session.

Relative output of power vs. non-power exercises

Power exercises are explosive, fluid, continuous in nature, and incorporate momentum. These are advanced exercises, and can result in severe injury if they are not performed correctly, or if you are not suitably conditioned for them.

The table above gives an indication of the outputs of power exercises relative to some non-power exercises:

Power exercise	Watts	Non-power exercise	Watts
Jerk	5400	Squat	1100
Snatch	3000	Dead lift	1100
Clean	2950	Bench press	300

CAUTION: Do not attempt the exercises in this section without proper instruction and supervision. They are not suitable for beginners, and should not be done if you have a pre-existing neck, back, or knee injury.

BENT LEG DEAD LIFT

Core exercise • Compound/multi-joint
• Pull • Close chain • Barbell
• Intermediate to advanced

The Dead Lift, among the most complete exercises, is one of three events in competitive Power-lifting (alongside the Bench Press and Squat). The aim is to lift the heaviest weight possible. The Dead Lift has a place in functional training and back rehabilitation regimes, and is an ideal preparation for the Power Clean and Jerk.

Basic description

Lift the bar by extending the knees and hips, using the combined strength of the back, hips, and thighs. Return and repeat.

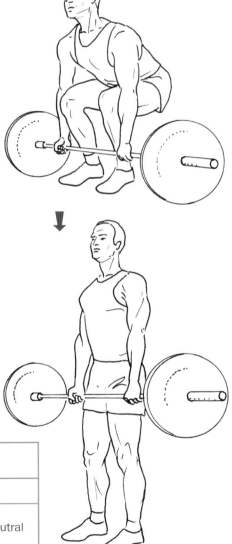

Tips for good form

· Get a proper demonstration and instruction before doing this exercise.
· Find good form before increasing weight.
· In the lift, lead with the head and shoulders; keep the hips low.
· Once the bar passes the knee, push the hips forward.
· Throughout the exercise, keep the bar close to the body.
· Try to keep the chest and shoulders open.
· Maintain posture stabilization throughout.
· Inhaling on the upward phase helps to increase intra-abdominal pressure, to keep the shoulders open, and prevent spinal flexion. Exhale on the downward movement.

STARTING POSITION

· Stand with feet shoulder-width apart and underneath the barbell.
· Squat down and grasp the bar with an alternate overgrip, (one hand over, one hand under).
· Grip width is shoulder-width or slightly wider.
· Keep posture aligned.

ANALYSIS OF MOVEMENT	JOINT 1	JOINT 2	JOINT 3
Joints	Knee	Hip	Spine
Joint movement	Up—extension Down—flexion	Up—extension Down—flexion	Up—extension Down—flexion to neutral
Mobilizing muscles	Quadricep group	Gluteus maximus Hamstring group	Erector spinae

ANATOMY FOR STRENGTH AND FITNESS TRAINING

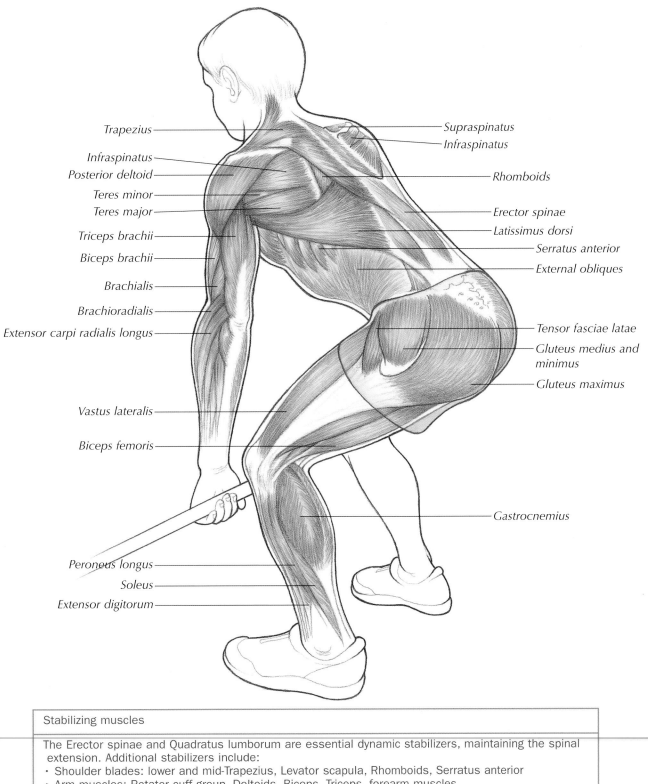

Trapezius

Infraspinatus

Posterior deltoid

Teres minor

Teres major

Triceps brachii

Biceps brachii

Brachialis

Brachioradialis

Extensor carpi radialis longus

Vastus lateralis

Biceps femoris

Peroneus longus

Soleus

Extensor digitorum

Supraspinatus

Infraspinatus

Rhomboids

Erector spinae

Latissimus dorsi

Serratus anterior

External obliques

Tensor fasciae latae

Gluteus medius and minimus

Gluteus maximus

Gastrocnemius

Stabilizing muscles

The Erector spinae and Quadratus lumborum are essential dynamic stabilizers, maintaining the spinal extension. Additional stabilizers include:
· Shoulder blades: lower and mid-Trapezius, Levator scapula, Rhomboids, Serratus anterior
· Arm muscles: Rotator cuff group, Deltoids, Biceps, Triceps, forearm muscles
· Trunk: Abdominal group
· Hips: Gluteus medius and minimus, Deep external hip rotators, Adductor group
· Lower leg: Ankle stabilizers, Tibialis anterior, Gastrocnemius

POWER CLEAN

Power exercise • Compound/multi-joint
• Pull • Close chain • Barbell
• Advanced

➡ The Power Clean forms the first phase of the Clean and Jerk (see also p136). You should master the individual phases before combining them into one exercise.

Basic description

Pull the bar up off the floor by extending the hips and knees. Using the upward momentum, as the bar reaches the knees, explosively raise the shoulders, keeping the barbell close to the thighs.

When the barbell reaches mid-thigh, jump upward, and thrust the hips forward, extending the body. This will accelerate the upward momentum of the bar. At this point, most of the work shifts from the legs and lower back to the upper back, shoulders, and arms.

As the bar moves past waist-height, pull the body underneath the bar, bending the elbows, and drop down onto a flat foot, so that you end into a half squat, with the barbell supported on the upper chest, and the elbows pointing forward. Stand up and stabilize.

Return by dropping the elbows and controlling the bar down to mid-thigh. From there, squat down to the starting position.

Tips for good form

· Get a proper demonstration and qualified instruction.
· Get good form before increasing weight.
· In the lift, lead with the head and shoulders.
· Do not jerk the weight, rise steadily, then accelerate. Generate the power into the legs and back, and then shift it fluidly to the upper back, shoulders, and arms.
· Throughout the exercise, keep the bar close to the body.
· Maintain posture stabilization throughout.
· Inhaling on the upward phase helps to increase intra-abdominal pressure, keeps the shoulders open, and prevents spinal flexion.

STARTING POSITION
· Stand with feet shoulder-width apart beneath the barbell.
· Squat down and grasp the bar with an overhand grip, slightly wider than shoulder-width.
· Pull shoulders back so they are positioned over the bar.
· Arch back slightly, pushing buttocks back.
· Extend arms.
· Keep posture aligned and stabilized.

ANALYSIS OF MOVEMENT	JOINT 1	JOINT 2	JOINT 3	JOINT 4
Joints	Ankle	Knee	Hip	Spine
Joint movement	Up—plantarflexion	Up—extension	Up—extension	Up—extension
Mobilizing muscles	Gastrocnemius Soleus	Quadricep group	Gluteus maximus Hamstring group	Erector spinae

ANALYSIS OF MOVEMENT	JOINT 5	JOINT 6	JOINT 7	JOINT 8
Joints	Shoulders	Scapula	Elbow	Wrist
Joint movement	Up—flexion, abduction, external rotation	Up—elevation, Upward rotation	Up—flexion	Up—extension
Mobilizing muscles	Deltoid, Supraspinatus, Infraspinatus, Teres minor Pectoralis major (clavicular aspect)	Upper Trapezius Levator scapula Serratus anterior	Bicep group	Extensor carpi radialis longus Extensor carpi radialis brevis Extensor carpi ulnaris

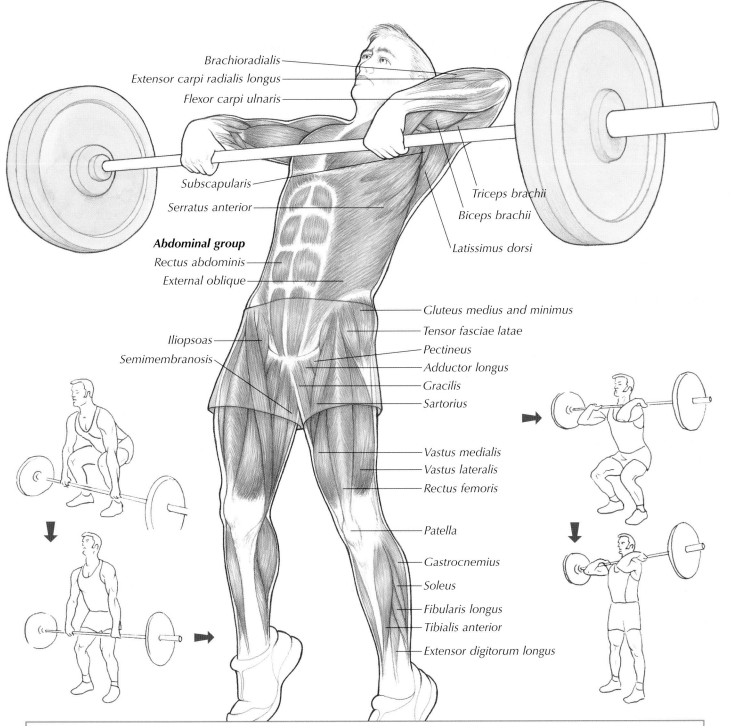

Brachioradialis

Extensor carpi radialis longus

Flexor carpi ulnaris

Subscapularis

Serratus anterior

Abdominal group

Rectus abdominis

External oblique

Iliopsoas

Semimembranosis

Triceps brachii

Biceps brachii

Latissimus dorsi

Gluteus medius and minimus

Tensor fasciae latae

Pectineus

Adductor longus

Gracilis

Sartorius

Vastus medialis

Vastus lateralis

Rectus femoris

Patella

Gastrocnemius

Soleus

Fibularis longus

Tibialis anterior

Extensor digitorum longus

Stabilizing muscles

The Erector spinae and Quadratus lumborum are essential dynamic stabilizers, maintaining the spinal extension.
Additional stabilizers include:
· Shoulder blades: Lower and mid-Trapezius, Levator Ssapula, Rhomboids, Serratus anterior
· Arms: Rotator cuff group, Deltoids, arm muscles
· Trunk: Abdominal group
· Hips: Gluteus group, deep external hip rotators, Adductor group
· Legs: Rectus femoris, Hamstrings
· Lower legs: Ankle stabilizers, Tibialis anterior, Gastrocnemius

PUSH JERK

Power exercise • Compound/multi-joint
• Push • Close chain • Barbell •
Advanced

➡ Olympic power-lifting is a competitive sport comprising two explosive lifts; the Clean and Jerk, and the Snatch (see p138). The Push Jerk is the second phase of the Clean and Jerk (see p134).

Basic description

Lower the body into a half squat. With rebound momentum, explosively accelerate upward with the legs, extending at the knee and hip. Shift this momentum to the arms and shoulders, pushing the barbell upward into an extended overhead position. Return the bar to the shoulders and repeat.

Tips for good form

· Get a proper demonstration and instruction before doing this exercise.
· Find good form before increasing weight.
· Keep the chest and shoulders open.
· Maintain posture stabilization throughout.

ANALYSIS OF MOVEMENT	JOINT 1	JOINT 2	JOINT 3
Joints	Ankle	Knee	Hip
Joint movement	Up—plantarflexion	Up—extension	Up—extension
Mobilizing muscles	Gastrocnemius Soleus	Quadricep group	Gluteus maximus Hamstring group

ANALYSIS OF MOVEMENT	JOINT 4	JOINT 5	JOINT 6
Joints	Elbow	Shoulder	Scapula
Joint movement	Up—extension	Up—flexion, abduction	Up—upward rotation
Mobilizing muscles	Triceps brachii Anconeus	Anterior and mid-deltoid Pectoralis major (clavicular aspect)	Serratus anterior

Stabilizing muscles	The Erector spinae and Quadratus lumborum are essential dynamic stabilizers, maintaining the spinal extension. Additional stabilizers include: · Shoulder blades: lower and mid-Trapezius, Levator scapula, Rhomboids, Serratus anterior · Arms: Rotator cuff group, Deltoids, and arm muscles · Trunk: Abdominal group · Hips: Gluteus medius and minimus, deep external hip rotators, Adductor group · Legs: Rectus femoris, Hamstrings · Lower leg: Ankle stabilizers, Tibialis anterior, Gastrocnemius

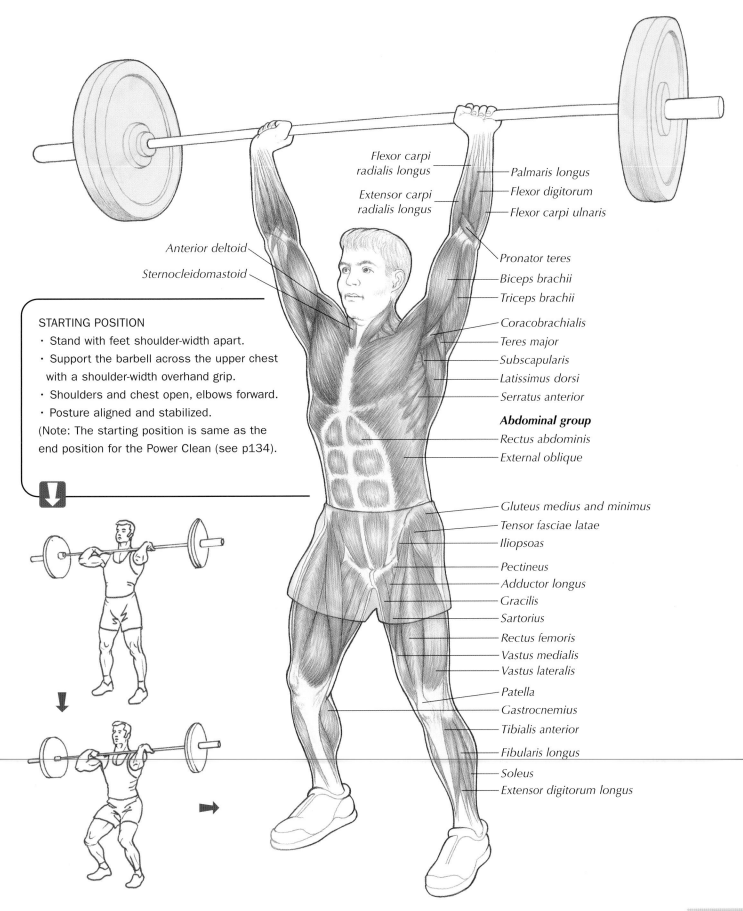

Flexor carpi
radialis longus

Extensor carpi
radialis longus

Anterior deltoid

Sternocleidomastoid

Palmaris longus

Flexor digitorum

Flexor carpi ulnaris

Pronator teres

Biceps brachii

Triceps brachii

Coracobrachialis

Teres major

Subscapularis

Latissimus dorsi

Serratus anterior

Abdominal group

Rectus abdominis

External oblique

Gluteus medius and minimus

Tensor fasciae latae

Iliopsoas

Pectineus

Adductor longus

Gracilis

Sartorius

Rectus femoris

Vastus medialis

Vastus lateralis

Patella

Gastrocnemius

Tibialis anterior

Fibularis longus

Soleus

Extensor digitorum longus

STARTING POSITION
· Stand with feet shoulder-width apart.
· Support the barbell across the upper chest
  with a shoulder-width overhand grip.
· Shoulders and chest open, elbows forward.
· Posture aligned and stabilized.
(Note: The starting position is same as the
end position for the Power Clean (see p134).

TOTAL BODY AND POWER EXERCISES

POWER SNATCH

Power exercise • Compound/multi-joint
• Pull • Close chain • Barbell
• Advanced

The appropriately named Snatch is a fast, synchronized lift that requires timing, muscle coordination, good conditioning, and excellent stability. It is a high-risk exercise, not to be practiced without proper instruction and supervision.

Basic description

Stand with feet shoulder-width apart, underneath the barbell. Squat down and grasp the bar with an overhand grip, roughly double shoulder-width. Pull the shoulders back until they are positioned over the bar. Arch the back slightly, pushing the buttocks back, and keep the arms extended.

Tips for good form

· Get good form before increasing weight.
· In the lift, lead with the head and shoulders.
· The snatch needs to be one coordinated, continuous movement executed with speed. Do not jerk the weight from the floor. Rise steadily, then accelerate. Generate power into the legs and back, and shift it fluidly to the upper back, shoulders, and arms.
· Maintain posture stabilization throughout.
· Inhale on the upward phase to help increase intra-abdominal pressure, keep the shoulders open, and prevent spinal flexion.

ANALYSIS OF MOVEMENT	JOINT 1	JOINT 2	JOINT 3	JOINT 4
Joints	Ankle	Knee	Hip	Spine
Joint movement	Up—plantarflexion	Up—extension	Up—extension	Up—extension
Mobilizing muscles	Gastrocnemius Soleus	Quadricep group	Gluteus maximus Hamstring group	Erector spinae

ANALYSIS OF MOVEMENT	JOINT 5	JOINT 6	JOINT 7	JOINT 8
Joints	Shoulders	Scapula	Elbow	Wrist
Joint movement	Up—flexion, abduction, external rotation	Up—elevation Upward rotation	Up—extension	Up—extension
Mobilizing muscles	Deltoid Supraspinatus Infraspinatus Teres minor Pectoralis major (clavicular aspect)	Upper Trapezius Levator scapula Serratus anterior	Up—extension	Extensor carpi radialis longus Extensor carpi radialis brevis Extensor carpi ulnaris

Stabilizing muscles	The Erector spinae and Quadratus lumborum maintain spinal extension Shoulder blades: lower and mid-Trapezius, Levator scapula, Rhomboids, Serratus anterior Arms: Rotator cuff group (very important), Deltoids, arm muscles Trunk: Abdominal group Hips: Gluteus medius and minimus, deep external hip rotators, Adductor group Legs: Rectus femoris, Hamstring group Lower leg: Ankle stabilizers, Tibialis anterior, Gastrocnemius

ANATOMY FOR STRENGTH AND FITNESS TRAINING

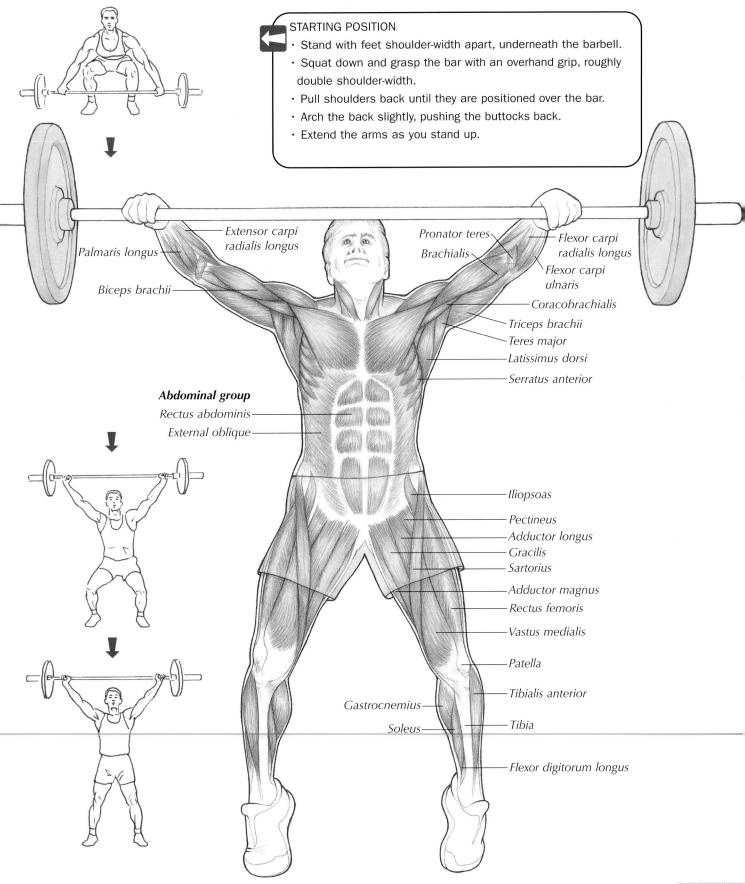

Extensor carpi radialis longus

Palmaris longus

Biceps brachii

Pronator teres

Brachialis

Flexor carpi radialis longus

Flexor carpi ulnaris

Coracobrachialis

Triceps brachii

Teres major

Latissimus dorsi

Serratus anterior

Abdominal group
Rectus abdominis
External oblique

Iliopsoas

Pectineus

Adductor longus

Gracilis

Sartorius

Adductor magnus

Rectus femoris

Vastus medialis

Patella

Tibialis anterior

Gastrocnemius

Tibia

Soleus

Flexor digitorum longus

TOTAL BODY AND POWER EXERCISES

GLOSSARY

Abduction Movement of a limb away from the center line, such as lifting a straight arm laterally from your side.

Adduction Movement of a limb toward the mid-line of the body, such as pulling a straight arm toward your side.

Agonist A muscle that causes motion.

Anterior (ventral) The front of the body.

Anatomical position Body upright, feet together, arms hanging at sides, palms facing forward, thumbs facing away from body, fingers extended.

Antagonist A muscle that moves the joint opposite to the movement produced by the agonist.

Auxiliary Optional exercise to supplement a core exercise. Auxiliary exercises place greater relative intensity on a specific muscle or on the head of a muscle.

Circumduction Circular movement (combining flexion, extension, adduction, and abduction) with no shaft rotation.

Compound exercises Involving two or more joint movements.

Concentric A muscle contraction, resulting in its shortening.

Core A principal exercise.

Closed chain An exercise in which the end segment of the exercised limb is fixed, or supporting the weight. Most compound exercises are closed-chain movements.

Distal Farther away from the center of the body.

Duration The number of sets or exercises for each specific muscle group. Duration may include number of repetitions.

Dynamic stabilizer A biarticulate muscle that simultaneously shortens at the target joint and lengthens the adjacent joint with no appreciable difference in length. Dynamic stabilization occurs during many compound movements.

Eccentric The contraction of a muscle during its lengthening.

Eversion Moving the foot away from the medial plane.

Extension Straightening, extending, or opening out a joint, resulting in an increase of the angle between two bones.

External rotation Outward (lateral) rotation of a joint within the transverse plane of the body. The resulting movement will be toward the posterior (back) of the body.

Flexion Bending a joint, resulting in a decrease of angle.

Frequency The number of workouts per week (or unit time) or number of times a muscle group is trained per unit time.

Functional An exercise that allows you to gain motor development or strength in the manner in which it is used in the execution of a particular task (eg: specific sport skill, occupational task, or daily activity).

Hyperextension Extending a joint beyond its normal anatomical position.

Inferior Movement away from the head.

Intensity The amount of weight used, percentage of one repetition maximum, or degree of effort used during exercise.

Internal rotation Inward medial rotation of a joint within the transverse plane of the body. Movement is directed toward the anterior (front) surface of the body.

Inversion Moving the sole of the foot toward the medial plane.

Isolated An exercise that involves just one discernible joint movement.

Isometric Contracting a muscle without significant movement; also referred to as static tension

Isotonic Muscle contraction with movement against a natural resistance.

Lateral Away from sagittal mid-line of body

Medial Toward sagittal mid-line of body

Open chain An exercise in which the end segment of the exercised limb is not fixed, or is not supporting the weight. Most isolated exercise are open-chain movements.

Posterior (dorsal) Located behind or to the back of the body.

Pronation Internal rotation of the foot or forearm.

Protrusion Moving anteriorly (toward the front).

Proximal Closer to the center or core of the body.

Push Movement away from the center of the body during the concentric contraction of the target muscle. Isolated movements are classified by their compound counterparts.

Pull Movement toward the body's center; opposite of push.

ROM Range of Motion. The amount of movement at each joint. Every joint in the body has a "normal" range of motion.

Rotation Circular (rotary) movement around the longitudinal axis of the bone.

Sagittal plane A division that separates the body into a left and a right half. Movements in the sagittal plane are in the forward-backward direction.

Synergist A muscle that assists another muscle to accomplish a movement.

Stabilizer A muscle that contracts with no significant movement.

Superior Above, on top, or toward the head.

Supination External rotation of the foot or forearm, resulting in appendage facing upwards.

Target The primary muscle intended for exercise.

Transverse plane Division separating the body into an upper and lower half. Movements in this plane are horizontal.

Weight-bearing exercise Any type of activity that causes the body to react against gravity.

INDEX

Page numbers in **bold** indicate references to illustrations.

INDEX

INDEX

RESOURCES

FURTHER READING

Wyatt, Tanya. *Be Your Own Personal Trainer*. New Holland, London, 2004.

Floyd, R.T. and Thompson, Clem W. *Manual of Structural Kinesiology* (14th ed.). McGraw-Hill Higher Education, 2003.

Delavier, Frédérick. *Strength Training Anatomy*. Human Kinetics, Illinois, 2001.

Various. *The Complete Guide to the Human Body*. Five Mile Press, Noble Park, Victoria, Australia, 2002.

Sudy, Mitchell (Supervising editor). *Personal Trainer Manual—The Resource for Fitness Instructors*. American Council on Exercise, 1991.

Steindler, Arthur. *Kinesiology of the Human Body*. Charles C. Thomas, 1964.

Dalgleish, J. and Dollery, S. *The Health and Fitness Handbook*. Pearson Education Limited. Essex. 2001.

Baker, Robert B. *Training with Weights: The Athlete's Free-weight Guide*. Sports Illustrated.

Baum, Kenneth and Trubo, Richard. *The Metal Edge: Maximize your sports potential with the mind/body connection*.

Muybridge, Eadweard. *The Human Body in Motion*. Dover Publications, New York, 1955.

McCracken, Thomas (General editor). *New Atlas of Human Anatomy*. Constable, London, 2001.

Viljoen, Wayne. *The Weight Training Handbook*. New Holland, London, 2003.

WEBSITES

www.anatomical.com Charts relating to anatomy, training heart rates, weight-training illustrations, alternative health therapies, health education, etc.

www.exrx.net Exercise Prescription on the Net is a free resource for exercise professionals, coaches, and fitness enthusiasts.

www.sportsci.org Although this is a very scientific site, there are some good articles on research relating to various sports and the issues affecting them, such as hydration, training, nutrition etc.

www.acefitness.org A good site covering all aspects of health, nutrition, and fitness. Although it deals mostly with the education of fitness practitioners, it also provides vast amounts of information for the layman.

www.fitnesszone.co.za An excellent site covering all aspects of health, fitness, and nutrition.

www.musclemedia.com Specifics regarding weight-training issues. Back orders of magazines are available, as well as information on nutrition specific to weight-training.

AUTHOR'S ACKNOWLEDGMENTS AND DEDICATION

The inner function and structure of the human body is a fascinating metaphor of life. In my studies of anatomy I've been privileged to have had many great teachers and students along the way. I hope they have enjoyed the journey as much as I have. Thank you to Dr Craig Bowker and Howard Morris, wherever you are now, for giving me the perfect introduction to a lifelong interest; to my colleagues Sally Lee and Tanya Wyatt, two of the best health and fitness professionals I am ever likely to know, for raising the bar; to artist James Berrangé, you made the words come alive; and to the team at New Holland, Alfred, Maryna, and Gill, for your support and commitment to the project, without you, this book would still be just a good idea.

Finally, to my late parents, I wish you could have seen this.